The No-Nonsense Guide to Hurricane Safety

Jeffery D. Sims

Books may be purchased by contacting the publisher and author at Lulu.com, Amazon.com, or contact the author at:

Beyond The Spectrum Books
http://beyond-the-political-spectrum.blogspot.com/

Cover Design: Jeffery D. Sims
Publisher: Lulu Books & Beyond The Spectrum Books
ISBN 978-1-304-73303-0
1. Reference 2. Science 3. Weather 4. Safety 5. Hurricanes
First Edition
Printed in North Carolina, USA

Acknowledgement

For my dad, for showing me (by example) that there is no freedom like working for yourself.

Table of Contents

Introduction

Simply put, in some ways I was a normal child while in other ways, I was anything but. It is the abnormal part of my being which accounts for why you are holding this book in your hot little hands (or reading it on your tablet). While I enjoyed watching cartoons, reading comic books, and favored science-fiction (notice a pattern?), I was also fascinated—infatuated actually—with learning about strange, unusual, and otherwise unexplained uncommon events. Whether the subject was verifying the legitimacy of alleged occurrences explored in the field of parapsychology, learning about what things exist beyond the boundaries of our planet through the area of astronomy, or—of relevance to you the reader—understanding the causes of interesting weather phenomenon like tornadoes and hurricanes.

As an adult, my love of learning had grown to encompass many other subjects, including history and politics (which I went to college to study). I had come to the awareness that I had/have an innate thirst for knowledge, about everything around me. As a result, I have more books than I will ever read, probably more than the average person. I've also probably had more different types of jobs than the average person. I've done a great deal of living. And in everything I've read, done, and observed, I've taken a great deal of awareness about life and the nature of the universe around us with me (yes, I know...a little grandiose, if not self-centered-sounding). I suppose by way of osmosis, I had also developed a love of teaching after having fallen into the vocation of substitute and adult education instructor. Because of these experiences, I have been driven to observe the world with an attempt to gain a deeper meaning of it all...and maybe bring a little bit of insight to others.

I am also driven to write about my observations –without the latent bias of emotion, beliefs, or cultural beliefs—in order to convey a semblance of truth (the "teacher" in me I suppose) and maybe give others a little something to think about. This is why I started blogging and writing regularly some years ago. In an indirect way, writing is also a way for me to help others to think about and offer possible solutions to grander problems posed by counterproductive policies and our own individual thinking. But it was only recently that I was motivated to combine my proclivity for (objective) observation, thirst for learning, and ultimately my writing to create a series of books based on my own intellectual curiosities and love for seeking solutions to existing problems.

This resulting compendium of interests and ideas has the (intended) benefit of imparting in those who chose to purchase and read it a level of awareness and knowledge about the an aspect of the dangers –those presented by the earth we live on—inherent in the world around us. And although there are no certain safe places to hide from real-life dangers, there *are* places as well as courses of actions that one can take to limit exposure to these dangers. I acknowledge this fact throughout the book(s) by using terms like *relatively*, *comparatively*, or variations of such words to convey that the suggestions offered are in, all likelihood based on research and other findings, the best options given the dangers and circumstances.

It is my hope that the information in this book (or as I call it, "safety manual") will save a life, or at least prevent serious injury to those who would might be affected by a related dangerous experience.

So without further ado, I present to you, the No-Nonsense Guide to Hurricane Safety...
--Jeffery D. Sims

Hurricanes

What Are They?

Actually, hurricanes are only one name for a particular type of large, intense wind-driven storm that forms over warm the ocean waters found slightly north or south the earth's equator (the area of the earth near the dividing line between the Northern and Southern Hemispheres). Generically known as *tropical cyclones*, a hurricane is a type of low-pressure weather system that forms over tropical or sub-tropical waters (hence the "tropical" in the generic name of these types of storms). These particular storms regularly organize around intense thunderstorm-related activity. Accompanied by torrential rains, they are distinguished by their strong *cyclonic* (rapid inward circulation of) surface winds around the storm's low-pressure center (the "cyclone"). The result is a destructive storm system that attacks coastal regions of land areas where they make *landfall* (the point when and where a storm over water begins to move over land).

Hurricanes are recognized by the distinctive shape of their structure, indicating their circular rotation as seen in weather satellites photos. This structure is indicative of their relatively large size as storms go (although their size can and does vary based on individual factors). In many cases, the destructive effects of a hurricane can extend out some hundreds of miles/kilometers from the storm's center.

A satellite image of Hurricane Irene off the coast of New York City in late 2011, illustrating the distinctive circular shape of a hurricane's cloud structure.

Hurricanes or tropical cyclones are known by different names, depending on the part of the world where they occur. For example, tropical cyclones are known as "hurricanes" in areas of the Western North Atlantic and eastern parts of the North Pacific oceans. They are also known by the same name when they form in or occur in the Caribbean Sea or in the Gulf of Mexico. But In the western part of the North Pacific Ocean, they are called "typhoons." In other areas, they are called "cyclones," "severe tropical cyclones," and yes, by their generic name—"tropical cyclones. "

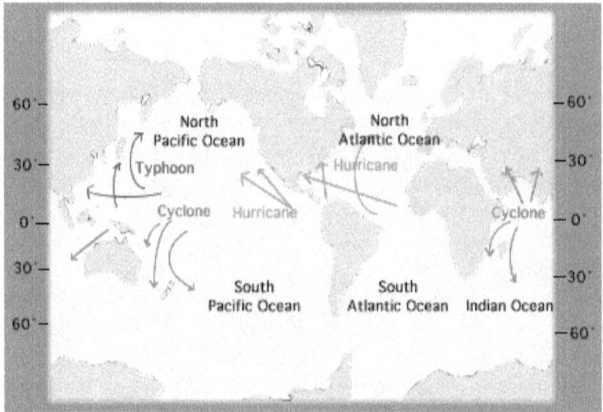

Depending on where they occur around the globe, tropical cyclones are known by different things.

Despite being called by several different names, hurricanes are dangerous storms of varying magnitudes, depending on the abundance (or scarcity) of the conditions needed to create them. But even weak hurricanes can be potentially damaging to property they ravage...and fatal for people in their paths who fail to take precautions to avoid the various dangers than accompany them.

The No-Nonsense Guide To Hurricane Safety

How Do They Form?

   The result of decades of research as well as advances in technology, scientists have a relatively firm understanding of the various elements that come together to form hurricanes—although the *exact* process by which a cyclone forms remains unknown. But for the majority tropical cyclones that move through the Atlantic region as hurricanes to eventually threaten areas of North America (the United States, Canada, Mexico, and Central America), their point of origin begins off the coast of the African continent. Most begin when air aloft is heated over the Sahara Desert (the largest "hot" desert in the world), and is carried by the strong winds of the *Easterly Jet Stream*[1] into the Atlantic Ocean. Once over the ocean, the heated air dips to the point where it is able to attract the moisture of the warm ocean waters through the process of evaporation, while it continues to travel. Once over the ocean, the now-semi-organized weather system begins to strengthen and grow, using a combination of the warm ocean waters and the spin of the Earth to fuel its existence (it is the spin of the Earth which contributes to a hurricane's spiral-shaped cloud formation, as well as its cyclonic wind structure).

   For both Atlantic-based hurricanes and other tropical cyclones—that is, storms which do not have their origins in weather systems that form off the western coast of Africa—that occur in other parts of the world, a certain number and level of factors need to be present for these storms to spawn. Under these particular conditions, the optimum atmospheric conditions can spur the organization of weather patterns that hurricanes are able eventually to form from. These factors include:

- Water that is at least 80 degrees F (26.6 Celsius).
- Relatively moist air
- Very warm surface temperatures
- A continuous evaporation and condensation cycle
- Wind patterns of varying directions that collide (converging winds)
- A difference in air pressure between the surface and high altitude

What these conditions allow is for the warmth of the ocean waters to provide enough heat and moisture as potential fuel for organizing weather systems to become tropical cyclones. The evaporation of the oceans' waters will usually combine with that heat and energy to spur this process on. Existing wind pattern near the oceans' surfaces will then cause the air to spiral air inward, creating bands of strong thunderstorms. These thunderstorms allow already warm air to warm even more, causing it to rise higher into the atmosphere. Stable higher-level winds aloft causes the organizing storm to grow stronger, causing a tropical cyclone to form. This is the process for organizing tropical cyclones that not only affect areas of North America and its vicinity as hurricanes, but also affect regions of the Eastern Pacific (also as hurricanes), as typhoons that affect the Western and Northern Pacific regions, and as cyclones that go on to affect areas of the South Pacific and Indian Oceans.

---

[1] Jet Streams are fast-moving patterns of air currents found at high altitudes (tens of thousands of miles/kilometers into the earth's atmosphere), which affects the various weather patterns around the globe. There are multiple jet streams found around the globe that affect weather patterns for the regions where the streams cross or shift over, such as the *polar jets*, and the *subtropical jets*. Meteorologists use the location of some of the jet streams as an aid in weather forecasting.

The No-Nonsense Guide To Hurricane Safety

Climatologists and weather forecasters have noted 4 distinct phases in the development of a hurricane/tropical cyclone. The 4 stages include:

- A *Tropical disturbance* occurs when warm air (e.g., that blown off the western coast of Africa into the Atlantic Ocean) dips over warm ocean waters. This causes the water vapor from the warm ocean to evaporate and condenses to the point where clouds form. The warmed air rises and is pulled into the clouds. As evaporation and condensation continues, the clouds start to build into high columns. A pattern develops, with the wind circulating around a center (the cyclonic wind-effect). As the moving column of air encounters more clouds, it becomes an active cluster of ocean-based thunderstorm clouds which forecasters call a *tropical disturbance*.
- The tropical disturbance will eventually become *a tropical depression* as the system matures. At this point, the thunderstorm cloud cluster grows higher and larger; the air at the top of the cloud column cools and becomes unstable. The cooling water vapor releases heat energy, causing the air pressure to rise and the winds to move out and away. The resulting surface pressure drop causes the air at the surface to move toward the lower pressure area and rise, creating even more thunderstorms. Winds in the storm cloud column spin faster and faster, whipping around in a circular motion. When the winds reach between 25 and 38 mph (40 and 61 km/h), the storm is called a tropical depression. When storms are beginning to take shape in the Atlantic Ocean, the United States' *National Hurricane Center*[2] will send out "hurricane hunters" (meteorologists and other specialized personnel who fly near or into cyclonic storms) to investigate whether the winds are blowing in a counterclockwise rotation in order to gauge its potential for strengthening .
- If the tropical depression continues to gather strength over the warm waters of the ocean that powers it, the wind speed of the storm will eventually reach 39 mph (62.76 km/h). At this point, the tropical depression becomes a *tropical storm*. This is also when meteorologists will name the storm to identify it during weather forecasts. The winds may continue to blow faster and begin twisting and turning around the eye's calm center. These winds of spin in a counterclockwise (west to east) direction (in the Northern Hemisphere and clockwise—east to west—in the Southern Hemisphere).
- A tropical storm officially becomes a tropical cyclone or *Hurricane* when the wind speeds reach 74 mph (119 km/h). As a full-fledged hurricane, the cloud columns of these storms area at a minimum 50,000 feet (15.24 kilometers) high and around 125 miles (201 km) across. The eye is ranges from around 5 to 30 miles (8 to 48 km) wide. The hurricane tends to travel along the route of the *trade winds* (prevailing surface winds found in the tropic regions of the planet) in a westerly direction, pushing the storm towards the Caribbean Sea, the Gulf of Mexico, or the southeastern coast of the U.S. Additionally, the winds and low air-pressure of a hurricane tends to cause high waves of ocean water to build up near the storm's eye, causing intense storm surges from increased tides when the storm makes landfall. Sometimes, all of the required elements for the formation of a hurricane (cyclone) aren't present. Under such circumstances,

---

[2] The National Hurricane Center (NHC), located in Miami, Florida, is a division of the United States' National Weather Service and is responsible for tracking, predicting, and measuring organizing tropical weather systems. It normally tracks storms that form and/or track within the region encompassing the northeast Pacific and the northern Atlantic Oceans.

this lack of storm ingredients forces the storm system to expend its limited energy, "blowing" itself out over open water before it fully develops. But when all the ingredients for hurricane

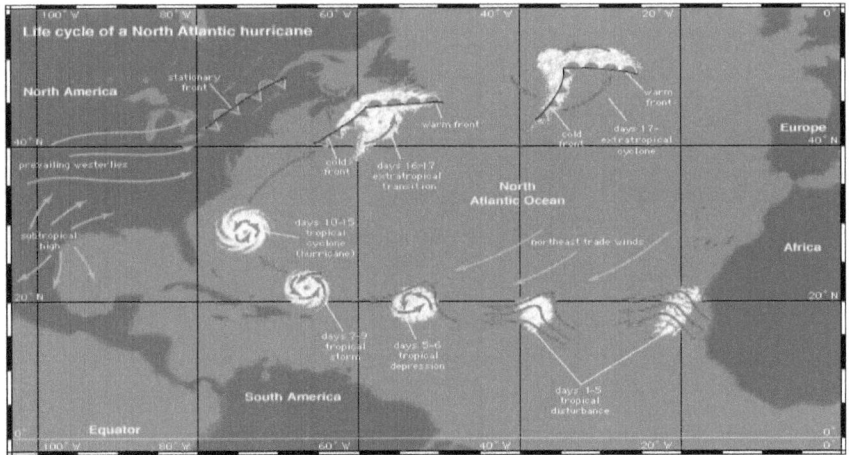

The evolution of an Atlantic hurricane as it travels across the ocean.

(cyclone) formation are present, the storm will continue to gather strength over the open warm waters of the ocean. As this happens, an "eye" begins to take shape in the center of the storm system.

The "eye" of a hurricane is a mostly circular area of light winds, little or no precipitation, and oftentimes fair weather found at the center of most tropical cyclones. Many times, blue sky or stars can be seen in the area of the storm's center eye region. This relative area of "calm" passing over populated areas is typically seen preceding the return of a hurricane's destructive winds, as the backside of the storm begins to travel over the storm's general path—and where we get the adage, "the calm before the storm." The infamy of this saying is partly buttressed by the fact that the eye of a tropical cyclone is typically surrounded by the storm's *eyewall*, a ring of towering columns of intense thunderstorms where most of the storm's most severe weather occurs. However, in weaker tropical cyclones, the eye is usually less-defined, and may be obscured by overcasts skies (and relatively high winds may extend well into the eye area as well). In lesser-organized cyclonic storms, an "eye" to speak of may not even form, replaced instead by an area of somewhat diminished winds but heavy rains. In all cyclones, however, the eye is the location of the storm's lowest levels of *barometric pressure* (the force of the weight of air has on a surface as it exerts pressure).

Fully-organized tropical cyclones (as well as strong tropical storms) also develop what are known as "rainbands" (or "outer rainbands"). These rainbands are composed of dense bands of thunderstorms that range in width from a few miles/kilometers to tens of miles/kilometers, and can be anywhere from a 50 to 300 miles (80 to 482 km) long. In some instances, the rainbands (like the eye) of a hurricane/cyclone can be obscured by higher level clouds, making it difficult for forecasters to use satellite imagery to monitor the storm. But most times, the bands themselves can easily be seen on satellite images of fully-developed hurricanes as spiraling cloud formation on their outermost perimeter. Rainbands can extend as much as a few hundred miles/kilometers from the center of these storms…but

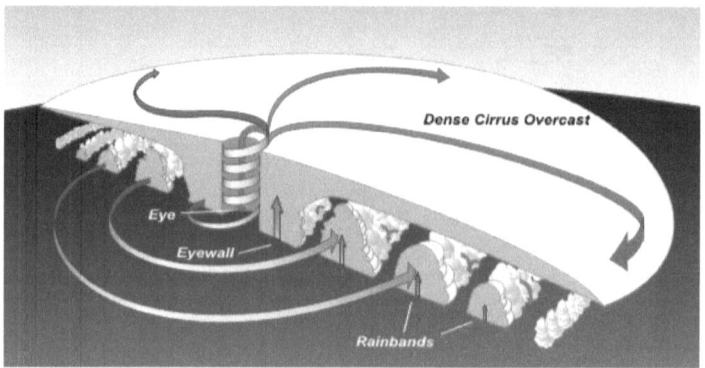

Cross-section of the interior wind mechanics of an active tropical cyclone/hurricane.

there are sometimes exceptions.   The rainbands of 1992's Hurricane Andrew—which notably decimated the city of Homestead, Florida—extended out only a mere 100 miles (160.9 km) out from the eye due to it being such a compacted hurricane, affecting a relatively small land area. Conversely, the rainbands of 1988's Hurricane Gilbert stretched over 500 miles (804 km) from *its* center.

As a maturing tropical cyclone, the winds of these storms tend to increase as they are fueled by the warm ocean waters. The column of thunderstorms embedded within begins to spend counterclockwise. This (fortunately) allows wind patterns to begin taking on somewhat familiar and predictable characteristics. As a hurricane moves, the wind on its right side blows in the direction of the storm's motion. The result is an increase in overall wind speed of the storm based on the storm's forward movement. To illustrate, a hurricane with sustained winds of 100 mph (160 km/h) and moving forward at a speed of 30 mph (48 km/h) has a combined wind of 130 mph on that particular side of the storm.

Conversely on the left side of the storm, the forward motion of 30 mph takes away from the opposing wind on the left side of the storm (100 mph- 30 mph - 70 mph [112 km/h]). This results in a 60 mph (96 km/h) differ-

Flying debris being drive by the winds of Hurricane Iniki on the Pacific island of Hawaii in 1992. Iniki was the most powerful hurricane to ever strike the island state.

ence in wind between each side of the hurricane. Naturally then, the right side of a hurricane usually has the fastest winds. While on the other hand, the left side often has the heaviest rain.

Once a fully-developed hurricane/tropical cyclone is formed, they begin churn forward over ocean waters as destructive storms. And depending on nearby prevailing weather conditions, the existence of other mitigating weather systems, and global wind patterns, hurricanes may move very slowly or quickly toward (populated) land areas— or even remain churning out over the ocean, never to make a landfall at all (these same factors may also indirectly affect the strengthening or weakening of an approaching hurricane). The varying factors affecting these storms' movement tends to occasionally cause them to travel forward in erratic patterns, which in turn causes difficulty forecasting when and where they might strike land.

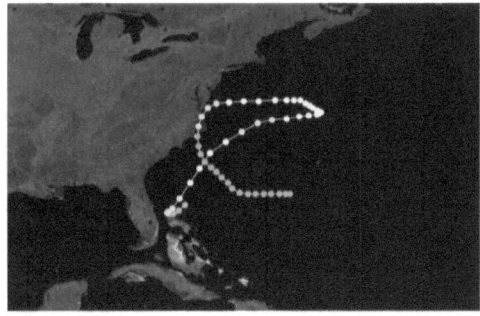

The erratic travel pattern of 1967's Hurricane Doria as it affected areas of the Eastern U.S. mainland.

Generally, the forward speed of a tropical cyclone varies, dependent on where in the ocean these storms form, and on which particular prevailing wind patterns they travel along. Overall though, the speed of a hurricane/cyclone is affected by its distance from the Earth's equator. The closer the storm is located to the equator, the slower its forward movement tends to be. But north of the equator, hurricanes/cyclones begin to increase in average forward speed. And although the average forward speed of an Atlantic hurricane is somewhat less than 20 mph (32 km/h), this can vary depending on individual and distinctive existing factors. The New England Hurricane of 1938 is estimated to have had the fastest forward ever speed for a hurricane at 70 mph (112 km/h).

What's more, a hurricane can dissipate (fall apart) during or before reaching any of its latter characteristic stages if all of the ingredients are not found at levels abundant enough to fuel the storm's strengthening. At these less-than-hurricane levels, these storms can be just as dangerous and potentially destructive as a full-fledged hurricane. In 2001, Tropical Storm Allison for example caused an estimated $9 billion in damage when it's erratic path took it first across the southeastern part of the state of Texas, then coastal and interior areas of Louisiana, and finally across areas of the Southeastern U.S. Lastly, once a hurricane moves over land, causing flooding and wind-driven destruction of property in populated areas, it tends to quickly lose its strength in the form of decreasing winds and driving rains. This is because the storm no longer has the warmth of the ocean waters to fuel its development. When this happens, the storm undergoes its developmental stages in reverse. If it becomes a minimum hurricane, it quickly weakens, going from a hurricane to a tropical storm, and from a tropical depression to a semi-organized weather system. In the event of a particularly powerful hurricane, the process dissolving the storm might take longer, resulting in the less-powerful aspects (tropical storms and depressions) of the cyclone to venture in farther inland and extending its path of destruction. This dynamic was seen firsthand when in 1954, Hurricane Hazel made landfall along the costal Carolinas in the U.S. The storm travelled north through several eastern American states before merging with another weaker storm system and striking the city of Toronto, Canada as an *extratropical storm*. [3]

---

[3] While over the Eastern U.S., Hurricane Hazel merged with an oncoming cold front in the region and turned on a northwest heading on a path towards Canada. When Hazel struck Toronto and areas of the Ontario province, it was still categorized as a category 1 (with winds in excess of 74 mph/119 kp/h). It caused some 81 fatalities, due mostly to massive flooding caused by the storm along local floodplains.

The No-Nonsense Guide To Hurricane Safety

What Makes Them Dangerous?

In most ways that matter, hurricanes could be described as being a "triple threat." Like most natural events of this magnitude, hurricanes carry with them inherent dangers caused directly by their direct impact on populated areas. But unlike other natural disasters, hurricanes bring with them multiple individual dangers from their 3 major destructive characteristics—heavy rains, high winds, and their propensity to spur other destructive weather-related phenomenon. Taken together, these individual hurricane attributes are capable of inflicting heavy casualties and widespread destruction, posing a particular level of danger to those who are immediately impacted by them.

Wind

Although hurricanes are somewhat noted for their exceedingly high sustained winds, wind itself is not as much the primary danger produced by these storms as the wind and water working in tandem to wreak havoc on populated areas. However, this does not mean to diminish the fact that the winds of a hurricane remain a major source (albeit indirect on some level) of potential death and destruction for those impacted by their landfall.

Wind is responsible for much of the structural damage caused by hurricanes. Depending upon the strength of a particular storm, these powerful winds are capable of uprooting trees, tearing down power lines, damaging or even destroying homes, or turning otherwise harmless objects into high-speed projectiles of potential lethal force. The maximum sustained winds from fast moving and powerful hurricanes may remain high, even when the storm has moved inland past the point of landfall. The winds of a hurricane range from 74 mph (119 km/h) in a *minimal hurricane* to greater than 155 mph (249 km/h) in a *catastrophic hurricane*.[4] However, these are documented wind speed ranges that have been measured at one time or another during these storms. In some rare instances, the winds of a hurricane/tropical cyclone can surpass the threshold of the minimum known wind speeds of the most powerful category of hurricane. This rare occurrence was observed during 1996's Severe Tropical Cyclone Olivia. According to meteorologists of the World Meteorological Organization (WMO), the highest non-tornado-related wind speed ever recorded was measured as a gust on April 10th. The 253 mph (407 km/h) gust was measured on Barrow Island, Australia during passage of the Category 4 cyclone's eyewall over the area. In the U.S., 1969's Hurricane Camille had the highest estimated wind speed at landfall ever documented (an estimated 190 mph/305 km/h) when it struck the country's Gulf Coast in the state of Mississippi. This particular storm's wind speed at landfall is also the highest ever documented for the entire planet.

The wind speed (and the resulting damage) caused by hurricanes can vary not only from cyclone to cyclone, but from one point in a single storm's path to the next. And because the wind speed of a hurricane is the chief indicator of the storm's strength and power, U.S.-based meteorologists have devised a scale which categorizes their strength based on each storm's sustained wind speed (wind speed over a set period of time).[5] This system of categorization, known as *The Saffir-Simpson Hurricane*

---

[4] During some particularly intense catastrophic hurricanes, accurate readings of high wind gusts during landfall are difficult to obtain because anemometers (wind-speed measuring devices) at reporting stations can be ripped from their foundations.

[5] The measurement of the "maximum sustained wind speed" of a tropical cyclone is not a universally-recognized one. This measurement differs from region to region. In the U.S. for example, the maximum sustained wind speed for a cyclonic storm is based on average wind speed

The No-Nonsense Guide To Hurricane Safety

Wind Scale, rates hurricanes on a scale from 1 to 5, based on wind speed and the known effects of sustained winds at certain levels speed.

Category	Wind Speed mph (km/h)	Description	
		*The Saffir-Simpson Hurricane Wind Scale*	
1	74-95 (119-154)	Minimal Hurricane	- Well-constructed frame homes could have roof damage. Large tree branches will snap and shallow-rooted trees may be toppled. Some flooding. Storm surges between 4-5 ft (1.2-1.5 meters).
2	96-110 (155-177)	Moderate Hurricane	-Well-constructed frame homes could sustain major roof and siding damage. Shallow-rooted trees will be snapped and/or uprooted. Possible damage to roadways. Coastal roads flooded out. Surges between 6-8 ft. (1.8-2.4 meters).
3	111-129 (178-207)	Major Hurricane	-Well-constructed framed homes may incur major structural damage, including to roofs. Many trees will be snapped or uprooted. Severe flooding. Surges between 9-12 ft (2.5-3.7 meters).
4	131-156 (210-251)	Major Hurricane	-Well-constructed framed homes sustain severe damage with loss of roof structures and/or some exterior walls. Most trees will be snapped or uprooted and power poles downed. Severe inland flooding. Surges between 13-18 ft (3.9-5.5meters).
5	157+ (252+)	Major Hurricane	-Well-constructed framed homes destroyed, with total roof failure and wall collapse. Many trees uprooted. Power poles sapped. Severe flooding farther inland. Surges greater than 18 ft (5.5 meters).

Similarly, meteorologists in other countries and in other regions throughout the developed world have established their own variation of the Saffir-Simpson Wind Scale. In some ways, these scales may differ, based on the differences in storm behavior (i.e. characteristics) in different parts of the world. However, the basic categorization of storm strength is somewhat standard for other similar scales. For example, the Japan Meteorological Agency (JMA) has its own scale measuring the relative strength of

Tropical Cyclone Intensity Scale (JMA) (For Sustained Winds of More Than 10-Minute Duration)	
Category	Wind Speed km/h (mph)
Typhoon	118+ (73+)
Severe Tropical Storm	89-117 (55-72)
Tropical Storm	62-88 (38-54)
Tropical Depression	Less than 61 (37)

over a period of 2 minutes, while in Japan and in other areas in the Far East, cyclones are measured in terms of sustained wind over a 10-minute period of time. Australia doesn't even use measured time as a criteria for measuring cyclones affecting its territorial region; the country's Tropical Cyclone Intensity Scale measures storm strength based on highest wind gusts.

approaching typhoons occurring in the areas of the East China Sea and the Western Pacific Ocean.

During a hurricane, homes, businesses, and other structures may be damaged or destroyed either directly by the storm's winds, or by wind-driven flying debris impacting these structures. Winds may also topple trees and power lines onto the top of homes and other buildings individuals might seek shelter in. Additionally, the winds of major hurricanes can rip the roofs off well-constructed homes, while causing relatively weak homes and buildings to crumble. Just as in tornadoes, mobile homes can easily be picked up by the storms' winds and tossed great distances, or even ripped apart completely. And debris such as signs, parts of buildings, and small items left outside become flying missiles in hurricanes. Placed within this context, the potential harm to people because of these winds becomes obvious. Being struck by fast-moving wind-driven objects—resulting in injury or even death, is a high probability in these storms. In some recorded instances, individuals have been killed as a result of high winds causing the structures they were in to collapse in around them. What's more, the winds generated by these storms can often remain above hurricane strength well inland, extending the area of the damage inflicted by these storms. Overall, **the damaging winds of a hurricane typically begin well before the strongest part of the storm (the eyewall) makes landfall.**

Water/Torrential Rainfall

Although the precise cause of death (and property damage) varies between these individual storms, water is the biggest single cause of death in a hurricane/tropical cyclone. More specifically, an estimated 90% of hurricane- and cyclone-related deaths and property damage result from what's known as *storm surge*. A storm surge is an abnormally high rise in water levels above the levels of normal astronomical tides[6] that accompanies a hurricane which makes landfall. Storm surges are produced by water being pushed toward the shore by the force of the winds moving cyclonically around hurricanes and other tropical weather systems. While most storm surges brought on by hurricanes making landfall tend to be between 6 and 12 inches (15 ¼ and 66 centimeters) above sea level, they can vary greatly between these average amounts; the storm surge accompanying 2005's Hurricane Katrina on America's Gulf Coast was estimated to have been between 25 and 28 feet (7.6 and 8.5 meters) above sea level.

Storm surges are dangerous because the combination of normal rising tide levels, and powerful cyclonic winds driving torrential rains and ocean waves onshore tends to bring with them heavy coastal flooding over large areas. Depending on the strength of a particular hurricane, storm surges can extend along several hundred miles/kilometers of open coastline, gradually diminishing away from the hurricane's center. And while the peak of most surges tend to occur primarily at the time of a hurricane's/cyclone's landfall, surges of significant force and height have been found to occur hours before) and/or after a storm's arrival on shore. The result is coastal flooding which can reach tens of miles/kilometers inland from the shoreline. The highest documented storm surge in the U.S. occurred in 2005 during Hurricane Katrina, when Pass Christian, MS, recorded a 27.8 foot storm surge above sea level. Globally, the highest storm surge ever reported was that produced by 1899's Cyclone Mahina, observed to have reached a height of at least 43 feet (13 meters) at Bathurst Bay, Australia.

---

[6] Astronomical tides are the rise and fall of sea levels caused by gravitational forces exerted by the Moon and the Sun, working with the rotation of the Earth.

The intensity of a hurricane's storm surge (as well as its potential for flooding affected areas) is strengthened or weakened by several different factors. The forward speed of a hurricane/cyclone and/or its overall strength is one such factor. For example, a powerful but fast-moving Category 4 or 5 hurricane making landfall might cause shorter-duration storm surges and more limited flooding than a slower-moving but Category 3 or 2. As a large and strong Category 3 storm, Hurricane Katrina caused catastrophic flooding due partly to intense storm surges along America's Gulf Coast when it made landfall because it moved relatively slow over the affected region. Comparatively speaking, 2004's

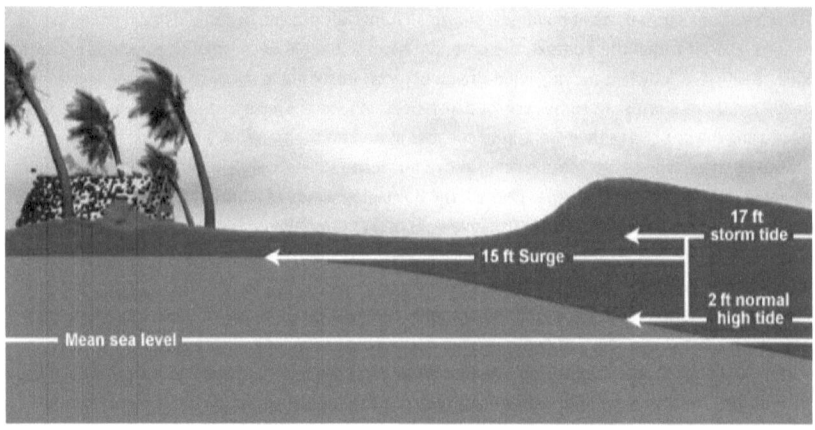

An illustration of the mechanics of a hurricane-driven storm surge as it makes landfall on a coastal area.

Hurricane Charley—a Category 4 storm—caused far less damage in the way of storm surge and flooding when it made landfall. This was because—despite its greater intensity—Charley moved over the affected area far faster than Katrina. Additionally, storms that make a perpendicular approach toward a coastline tend to cause a greater storm surge (and flooding) due to the impact of it direct angle. Conversely, hurricanes travel parallel to a coastline will produce a reduced storm surge. Other factors that affect storm surge (and flooding) include the intensity of a particular storm, landfall location, and the physical geography of a landfall location. These are factors which may be conveyed to the public during forecasts of an approaching hurricane, and whereby viewers can get a better understanding of the dangers involved when making preparations. **Storm surge is the singles greatest threat to life and property in a hurricane.**

Although the phenomenon of storm surge is directly related to much of the flooding that normally occurs during a hurricane, it is not exclusively so. Flooding is also a by-product of the torrential rains which accompanies a hurricane. Not only are these intensely heavy rains capable of inflicting major flooding on the areas around a storm's landfall, but can (and often do) bring a potentially equal amount of flooding to areas as many as hundreds of miles/kilometers from the area of initial impact. During a hurricane's/cyclone's initial landfall, rainfall amounts totaling anywhere from 5-10 inches (0.12 - 0.25 meters) are not unheard of (although these amounts can be higher depending on variables among individual storms). As in the case of associated storm surges, rainfall amounts can increase or decrease depending on the forward speed of a hurricane; slower-moving storms mean heavier rain amounts while faster-moving storms don't allow time for rain amounts to accumulate as much.

As the storm moves further inland and is downgraded to a tropical depression, the continued circulation, tropical moisture, and strength of the storm can combine to (continue to) bring heavy amounts of rain, particularly to places along the downgraded storm's path miles/kilometers away from the point of initial landfall. This accumulation of water in areas away from coastal flooding caused by storm surges creates what's known as "inland flooding." The potential for inland flooding is an often underestimated aspect of hurricanes by those who live near or even a moderate distance from the storm's point of initial landfall. The fact is that inland flooding from hurricanes accounts for many deaths from tropical cyclones. Hurricane Floyd for example, brought with it concentrated rains and record flooding to the Eastern U.S. during its track across the region back in 1999. Of the total number of 56 people who were killed as a result of the hurricane, 50 drowned due to inland flooding. Heavy flooding can also occur from less-than-full strength tropical weather systems such as tropical storms and tropical depressions.

In addition, flash flooding is also a possibility in many hurricanes. River and streams can quickly overrun their banks with little or no warning. Roads and bridges can and *are* often washed away by flash flooding, possibly resulting in individuals being cut off from escape routes...or even being swept away in fast-moving flood currents. The same potential problem can arise if roads and/or bridges become blocked by debris that is sometimes washed away from their original points of origin.

Other Weather-Related Threats

When hurricanes (and tropical storms) make landfall, they bring with them several life-threatening dangers. In addition to storm surges, flooding, and the dangers inherent within their powerful cyclonic winds, hurricanes tend to spawn added threats. The most relevant of these threats are tornadoes.

Tornadoes pose such an active threat during the height of a hurricane's landfall and during the weakening phases of these storms because—in the same way to warm ocean waters for active tropical weather systems—hurricanes /tropical cyclones provide all the necessary ingredients for tornadoes to form. Once a hurricane makes landfall, the storm often weakens without the "fuel" of warm ocean waters and the moisture they provide. This weakening means that the winds near the surface begin slowing down. At the same time the conditions for tornado formation begin to build, utilizing the momentum of winds aloft, hurricane-created wind shears, and alternating swirling winds—wind vortices that may become flipped vertically, creating tornadoes.

Hurricane-spawned twisters can affect areas many hundreds of miles/kilometers away from the hurricane itself. However, most occur within 150 miles (241 kilometers) of the point of landfall. These tornadoes usually form within the swirling bands of thunderstorms embedded with the outer rainbands typically in the "front-right quadrant" of the storm. In other words, if the storm is moving north, you're most likely to find tornadoes to the northeast of the cyclone's eye. And although hurricane-spawned tornadoes tend to be less powerful than those which form from supercell thunderstorms or active squall lines, they still represent the same levels of dangers from those created seen throughout America's "tornado alley." In fact, hurricane tornadoes can be particularly dangerous because quite often, many people fail to realize a tornado has formed until *after* the parent storm has passed. They do not always appear on weather monitoring systems, often striking without warning—and are thus harder to predict than their traditional supercell cousins. Researchers who study storms and storm damage are often not even aware that a tornado has even touched down until they survey the hurricane's damage and recognize the tell-tale signs of a tornado (such as a narrower damage path). Generally, the more intense a hurricane is in terms of categorical strength, the greater the tornado threat.

If a hurricane (or its lesser remnants) happens to pass over a hilly, mountainous region, or a coastal area composed of coastal bluffs, it could trigger dangerous and potentially landslides. The sometimes lengthy duration of heavy rains associated with these storms tend to cause an over saturation of the ground. This oversaturation of the ground, combined with the slope of the land and the particular geography of uneven terrain all play major roles in triggering landslides. These landslides can be relatively minor, causing property damage to a single concentrated area, or cause widespread destruction and/or loss of life. Category 5 Hurricane Camille virtually destroyed the coastline of the state of Mississippi when it ravaged the U.S. Gulf Coast region back in August of 1969. As a reduced Camille moved farther inland away from the coastline, heavy rains of an extended duration followed it, leading to heavy flooding, which caused landslides in Virginia. In 2011, Hurricane Irene and Tropical Storm Lee caused damaging landslides in the Chesapeake Bay area of the Eastern U.S. More catastrophic landslides as a result of Hurricane Mitch in 1998 affected large areas of the countries of Honduras, Nicaragua, Guatemala and El Salvador. During the landfall of *this* particular Atlantic-originating hurricane, massive landslides (along with flooding) resulted on an estimated 18,000 deaths occurring in the aforementioned Central American states.

One some occasions, successive hurricanes/typhoons will track along the same path in the same general area of a particular ocean region. These duel (or even multiple) hurricane and hurricane-related storm systems can either strike different land areas simultaneously, or follow one behind the other during some particularly active years. During a single week in August of 2004—within a few days each

A satellite image of 2 typhoons (Typhoons Parma & Melor) occurring simultaneously in the Western Pacific near the Philippines, in 2009.

other— Tropical Storm Bonnie and Hurricane Charley formed in the western Atlantic Ocean region. These two storms followed a similar track, sweeping across the Gulf of Mexico in succession. Tropical

Storm Bonnie made landfall on the coast of Florida's "panhandle" region and subsequently dissipated. Hurricane Charley, however, was strengthened by the warm waters and the unstable atmospheric conditions left in the wake of Tropical Storm Bonnie. It eventually made landfall in a densely populated area.

Trees that are uprooted or snapped trees by hurricane can be a constant threat to both life and/or property. This threat is often present before, during, and even after a hurricane has actually run its course. During Hurricane Sandy in 2013 a university graduate student was killed by a tree that crashed into his New York City home during the height of the storm. By contrast, the winds generated by the outer rainbands of Hurricane Ike (2011) were responsible felling a tree limb that killed a 10-year-old child nearly a day before the storm made actual landfall. A full 4 days after the hurricane passed, a utility worker was struck and killed by a tree branch weakened by the storm. Hurricane Ike went on to strike the U.S.'s western Gulf Coast region).

Finally, in addition to these specific weather-related threats, various other post-hurricane hazards can jeopardize both the health and lives of those affected by these storms. Some of these hazards are directly related to the weather, while others are indirectly so. For a detailed description of these threats, see the section under the section "After A Hurricane."

Tracking And Forecasting Hurricanes/Tropical Typhoons

Hurricane forecasting is reliant upon analyzing a great amount of data. Much of this data is the result of measurements taken by meteorologists utilizing various instruments. Space-based satellites capture infrared images of weather systems are used to collect information about a hurricane's position, wind movement, and the air temperature and moisture levels near the storm—all of which fuels them. These images often display as the colored time-lapsed animated "loops" that often air on news-based weather forecast segments (see below). Hurricane-hunter aircraft fly into hurricanes, collecting information about and measuring barometric pressure and wind intensity. Ocean-based buoys and other floating measuring instruments gather data about ocean currents, waves, and interactions between the sea and

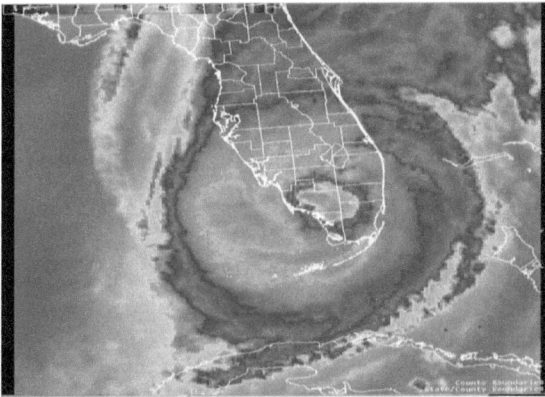

the atmosphere. Finally, land-based radar measures hurricane wind fields, monitor rain intensity, and tracks storm movement. But technology, as it relates to hurricane forecasting is far from full-proof. Much of the data collected by these instruments is analyzed and assimilated into computer-generated numerical prediction models. In the U.S., these computer prediction models are compared and to and often added to the computations used by European forecast models for

An infrared satellite image of Hurricane Wilma (2005) over the state of Florida

tracking and monitoring Atlantic-based hurricanes. This is because European government meteorological agencies tend to use faster computers, with better computational capacity than those used in the U.S. This makes them (arguably) somewhat more statistically accurate at predicting, say, the particular path (track) a hurricane located over the ocean might take as it heads towards land than those used by American meteorologists. And use of multiple predictive computer models often leads to conflicting weather forecasts of approaching hurricanes insomuch as where they may (or may not) make landfall.

Other on-going shortcomings in the overall understanding of—and ability to predict, with greater accuracy—hurricanes can add to the potential danger whenever these storms threaten landfall in populated regions. One of these shortcomings, related to the use of predictive computer models, is the inability of meteorologists to predict hurricane intensity (this is to say that hurricane intensity can be measured, but not predicted). This inability to predict hurricane intensity means that these storms can (and often do) suddenly intensify in terms of both wind speed and overall power; this can lead to forecasters giving inaccurate information about the expected potential impact in areas of landfall. This in turn, could lead to affected individuals underestimating the danger posed by approaching storms.

Finally, there is also a lack of an established warning system for the primary cause of death in Atlantic hurricanes. Specifically, there is no systematic warning system for the deadly storm surges that occur along the coasts where hurricanes make landfall. This lack of a warning system, aside from anticipatory forecasts, is also a reality for areas inland where storm surges can often extend—despite the relative lag in time from a storm's landfall to when it begins to move inland from the coast. Regardless of the decades-long shrinkage of the number of deaths caused by hurricanes, the increased understanding of their complex makeup, and advancements in meteorology, hurricanes/tropical cyclones still remain dangerous storms. They result in hundreds of lives lost worldwide, and billions of dollars in property damage annually.

The No-Nonsense Guide To Hurricane Safety

Where (and When) Do Hurricanes Occur?

Where do hurricanes/tropical typhoons occur is not a question with a simple cut-and-dry answer. They tend to form in different parts (i.e., ocean waters) around the world, during different periods of time. And based on the availability of optimal conditions which tend to fuel their formation, these storms may travel great distances from their points of origins. Generally, hurricanes/tropical cyclones tend to form within seven separate ocean regions across the globe, generally about 300 miles (480 km) north or (rarely) south of the equator. Each of these cyclone origin regions (as it were) have distinct characteristics which create different conditions related to hurricane/cyclone formation. For example, some ocean regions are more active than others insomuch as experiencing cyclonic storms, while others have lengthier windows of time in which tropical cyclones may occur during the year.

The general timeframe during the year for when hurricanes/tropical cyclones are most likely to form is known as *hurricane season* by weather forecasters. What's more, each ocean region has its own seasonal patterns. But worldwide, hurricane/tropical cyclone activity peaks in late summer (when the difference between the upper air temperatures and those of the various ocean' surfaces temperatures is the greatest). Globally, May is the least active month, while September is the most active month for these storms. Specifically, the various "hurricane seasons" for the 7 major ocean regions where these storms occur are as follows:

The Various Cyclone-Prone Ocean Regions & Their Related Peak Seasonal (Average) Activity Windows
North Atlantic Ocean   Hurricane season: June 1 - November 30. The most active period runs from about mid-August through the latter part of October. Locations that may be affected are the Caribbean, Bermuda, Central America including eastern Mexico, the eastern and Gulf coasts of the United States, and eastern Canada.
Eastern North Pacific Ocean   Hurricane season: May 15 - November 30. This is the second most active region for tropical cyclones in the world. These storms mostly move into the open eastern Pacific Ocean but can affect western Mexico and sometimes after developing, Hawaii.
Northwest Pacific Ocean   Typhoon season: All year. This is the most active basin in the world. Most typhoons form between July through November. The tropical cyclones that form here can affect the Philippines, southeast Asia including China and Taiwan, and Japan.
Arabian Sea   Severe Cyclonic storm season: April 1 - December 30. This basin has a double maximum because of the monsoon trough moving through at two different times of the year. Maximums occur from mid-April through May and from mid-September through mid-December.
Southwest Pacific Ocean   Severe Tropical Cyclone Season: October 15 - May 1. These tropical cyclones may affect eastern Australia.
Southeast Indian Ocean   Severe Tropical Cyclone Season: October 15 - May. These tropical cyclones may affect northern and

western Australia. This basin has a double maximum in mid-January, and mid-February through early March.

Southwest Indian Ocean
Tropical Cyclone Season: October 15 - May 15. These tropical cyclones may affect Madagascar and southeastern Africa. A double maximum occurs in mid-January and mid-February through early March.

As the chart indicates, hurricanes/tropical cyclones tend to form, gain strength, and travel over certain oceanic regions and—provided they don't remain out at sea—make landfall over costal lands within these regions. On average, approximately 85 hurricanes, cyclones, and typhoons form in the world's ocean waters every year. The waters of the Western North Pacific (including the South China & Philippine Seas) have the highest instance of storm activity; about 30% of the world's tropical cyclones occur in this region. The regions of the Eastern Pacific Ocean have the 2nd highest rate at 15%. The Western Atlantic Ocean, parts of the South & North Indian Oceans and the South Pacific Ocean come in at 12% of the world's total tropical cyclones. And the waters around Northern and Western Australia experience about 7% of these storms annually.

In the U.S., the land areas most vulnerable to hurricanes include the coastal regions along the East and Southeast Coasts, lands adjacent to the waters along the Gulf of Mexico, the entire chain of the Hawaiian Islands, and U.S. island territories in the Atlantic and Pacific Oceans (e.g., the islands of Puerto Rico, Guam, etc.). Making such areas even more vulnerable is the fact that some hurricanes that may eventually strike these vulnerable areas of the U.S. mainland can form in ocean waters relatively close to the coastal regions, allowing only a limited amount of time for preparations for those in potentially affected areas. Hurricanes that form in the Western Caribbean or in the Gulf of Mexico can form and move relatively quickly toward the Southern coastal waters of the country. What are more, inland

Coastal land regions in the continental United States most vulnerable hurricanes.

20

regions not far from the various coastal regions are vulnerable to the tropical storms and tropical depressions that these storms devolve into as they lose strength away from the "fuel" of the warm coastal waters. Various infrastructure and weak contingency plans of areas within these regions contribute to their increased vulnerability to the worst effects of these storms.

In 2006, the International Hurricane Research Center at Florida International University in Miami released a list of the 10 most areas of the mainland U.S. most vulnerable to hurricanes. The research comprising this list was based on specific criteria, including flooding potential, and flood-control measures, and the capabilities of state and local governments to respond to major hurricane events. Inherent in this list is the fact that these areas have all at one time experienced the most catastrophic levels of these tropical storms. In terms of the most vulnerable areas to the least, this list includes:

1. New Orleans, Louisiana
2. Lake Okeechobee, Florida
3. The Florida Keys
4. Coastal Mississippi
5. Miami/Ft. Lauderdale, Florida
6. Galveston/Houston, Texas
7. Cape Hatteras, North Carolina
8. Eastern Long Island, New York
9. Wilmington, North Carolina
10. Tampa/St. Petersburg, Florida

That 4 Florida regions are on this list reflects the reality that 40% of hurricanes that make landfall in the U.S. do so in that state. New Orleans ranked at the top of this list due to its then-recently rebuilt protective levees destroyed as a result of 2005's Hurricane Katrina (and where some 80% of the city was flooded due to broken levees breaches). Since the initial composition of this list, the order of the areas vulnerable to hurricanes have changed based on strengthening (or weakening criteria), but the areas themselves remain on the list as being the most susceptible to the destructive effects of these tropical storms. The history that some of these vulnerable regions have with the devastating impact of major hurricanes reflects their recognition as being particularly vulnerability to the force of these storms.

In the first year of the 20th century, the city of Galveston, Texas was destroyed by the deadliest single natural disaster to strike the U.S.—the Galveston Hurricane of 1900 (September 8th, 1900). The fact that so many died and so many buildings and homes were destroyed was due to several factors. First, the city itself (with a population of 37,000 people in 1900) was established on a shallow barrier island right off the mainland coast of the state of Texas. Second, the city was exposed to the Gulf of Mexico because of its position as a natural harbor situated on Galveston Bay. This reality was the result of the city being only 8.7 feet (2.7 meters) above sea level at its highest point at the time of the storm. What's more, the island had no sea wall to serve as a barrier against high tides and low-level flooding—despite its just-above-seal-level position. These physical features of the city made it vulnerable to the 15 foot (4.6 meter) storm surges that ravaged the island during the height of the storm's rampage through the region. Lastly, the technology—or lack thereof—of the time made it impossible to accurately track and/or to warn residents of the approaching disaster. Both weather forecasting and instant communication over distances were in their infancy at the time. For the most part, officials at the U.S. Weather Bureau's central officer in Washington D.C. could not even be made aware that s storm was even active until ships encountering a hurricane at sea put into harbor.

By the time the hurricane had travelled to the vicinity of the island city, it was too late for many of the residents to evacuate to an area of relative safety. Although the exact figures from the storm can never be known, the storm was estimated to have killed approximately 8,000 people—with some figures ranging as high as 12,000. This discrepancy is due to the loss of more accurate figures over time from the period, as well as the fact that many bodies were never recovered. In many cases, individuals had been washed out to sea. So many of the city's residents had been killed that burying the bodies was impossible; bodies found were immediately burned for many weeks after the storm's rampage. More people were killed in the Galveston Hurricane than the total of those killed in all the hurricanes that have struck the United States since.

Hurricane Katrina-caused flooding (2005) in the northwest area of New Orleans & nearby Metairie.

In more recent times, 2005's Hurricane Katrina—although not as deadly—proved to be the costliest natural disaster to ever strike the country. The destruction and mass casualties that the hurricane inflicted on the Gulf Coast region, particularly in the historic city of New Orleans, revealed that weak or extensive pre-parations can't fully protect populated areas from even the most predictable dangers associated with these storms. Despite contingency planning, the elaborate construction of flood channels/canals, water pumping stations, levees, and advanced warnings systems, some 1,800 people *still* perished both during the height of, and in the immediate aftermath of the catastrophic storm. Even more horrendous is the fact that Hurricane Katrina—for all the damage and destruction inflicted on the Gulf Coast region—was *only* a strong Category 3 (major) hurricane—not even the strongest category of tropical storms.

The No-Nonsense Guide To Hurricane Safety

What to Be On The Alert For...

Because of their tendency to form out over warm ocean waters (away from land), Hurricanes can be tracked from a distance by weather satellites as well as other means. Because they can be tracked easily and are routinely monitored by meteorologists as they develop, warnings of any anticipated landfalls in populated areas is usually advanced enough to allow affected individuals to evacuate to alternative locations of relative safety. This is a far different reality than that which held from over a century ago, when our basic lack of understanding about hurricanes as well as our technological limitations con-tributed to the inability to provide advanced warnings. But the advanced warnings given today, communicated by television, radio, and even the internet are just about all the alert that most people need in order to make preparations to facilitate their safety. And when conditions point to the possibility that *any* tropical storm system such as a hurricane might make landfall, weather-reporting agencies like the National Hurricane Center will issue certain weather advisories to alert potentially affected populations.

A *tropical storm watch* will be issued whenever weather conditions favor a possible threat to specified coastal areas by a tropical storm system with sustained winds of anywhere from 39 to 73 mph (63 to 117 km/h), and accompanied by heavy rains within a period of 48 hours. This particular weather advisory is also (sometimes) issued after an actual hurricane has made landfall, and has traveled far enough inland to the point where its predicted sustained wind speeds will fall below those of minimum hurricane level of (74 mph / 119 km/h).

A *tropical storm warning* is issued whenever weather conditions indicate the imminent landfall of a tropical storm-level weather system that is predicted to affect specified coastal areas within a period of 36 hours. Tropical storm warnings are also issued whenever a hurricane is expected to fall below minimum strength level, and the remaining below-hurricane storm system is predicted to affect areas inland along its path of travel.

A *hurricane watch* is issued whenever the potential for a hurricane of hurricane-level conditions (sustained winds of 74 mph / 119 km/h or higher) are possible within a specified coastal and adjacent inland areas. Hurricane watches are generally issued some 48 hours ahead of the predicted arrival of tropical storm-level winds, which invariably precede hurricane-strength winds. This relatively lengthy window of warning time is a means to give those potentially in the path of an approaching storm time to prepare by way of either evacuation or other pre-hurricane contingency plans; hurricane preparedness become difficult once wind speeds reach tropical storm force.

A *hurricane warning* is issued when a hurricane with sustained winds greater than minimum hurricane strength are expected within the watch area within a 36-hour period. This is an increased state of alert, as it indicates a greater certainty that a hurricane landfall expected. A hurricane warning can remain in effect when wind-driven high water (or a combination of dangerously high water and exceptionally high waves) presents a continual threat to life and property—even if the winds may have subsided below that of hurricane-level strength.

In addition to the system of weather watches and warnings issued by the NWS, there is another more traditional system of weather warnings for those residing in coastal areas, particularly in the U.S. Although this century-old practice was discontinued by the NWS in 1989, the Costal Warning Display Program was reestablished in the mid-2000s under the control of the U.S. Coast Guard. Currently, the

Coast Guard oversees this 100-year-old system that involves the displaying "storm flags" along the nation's shorelines to give warnings of heavy winds and/or other potentially dangerous storms. This system is based in part on the Beaufort Scale, a system of estimating and reporting wind speeds based on their observable effects on the environment.

Beaufort number	Wind Speed (mph)	Seaman's term		Effects on Land
0	Under 1	Calm		Calm; smoke rises vertically.
1	1-3	Light Air		Smoke drift indicates wind direction; vanes do not move.
2	4-7	Light Breeze		Wind felt on face; leaves rustle; vanes begin to move.
3	8-12	Gentle Breeze		Leaves, small twigs in constant motion; light flags extended.
4	13-18	Moderate Breeze		Dust, leaves and loose paper raised up; small branches move.
5	19-24	Fresh Breeze		Small trees begin to sway.
6	25-31	Strong Breeze		Large branches of trees in motion; whistling heard in wires.
7	32-38	Moderate Gale		Whole trees in motion; resistance felt in walking against the wind.
8	39-46	Fresh Gale		Twigs and small branches broken off trees.
9	47-54	Strong Gale		Slight structural damage occurs; slate blown from roofs.
10	55-63	Whole Gale		Seldom experienced on land; trees broken; structural damage occurs.
11	64-72	Storm		Very rarely experienced on land; usually with widespread damage.
12	73 or higher	Hurricane Force		Violence and destruction.

The Beaufort wind force scale

These flags, measuring 36 inches by 36 in. (91 centimeters by 91 cm.) are red in color and convey specific dangers in open coastal waters when they are hoisted and displayed—seen mostly during hurricane season. When one of these red flags are hanging, that warns those in and around the coastal waters that a storm warning has been posted such as a tropical storm—with the expectation of winds measuring between 55-73 mph (88 - 117 km/h) likely within 24 hours. When two flags are hoisted, one below the other, this means a hurricane warning is in effect. A hurricane warning means winds equal or greater than 74 mph (119 km/h) are likely within 24 hours.

In addition to storm flags, pennants are also used to indicate additional marine advisories. These pennants may be hoisted at different times along coastlines as a hurricane or tropical storm makes an approach toward landfall (and as weather conditions begin to deteriorate upon the storm's approach). A single pennant indicates a small-craft advisory that alerts those in and around coastal waters that weather, potentially dangerous to small crafts is either occurring or is forecast. Dangerous conditions include rough seas and increased winds of between 28-38 mph (45 - 61 km/h). When two pennants are hoisted, one below the other, a gale warning is in effect and is issued when winds blow between 39-54 mph (62-102 km/h). To distinguish the more imperative storm threats, the flags indicating the latter

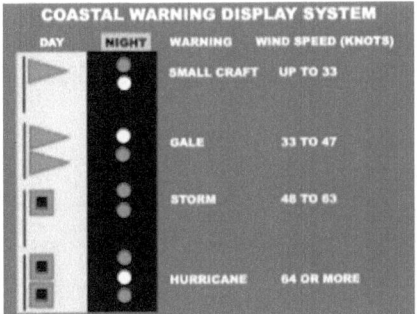

The system of flag warnings for the Costal Warning Display Program

two categories of storms come printed with small black squares printed on their faces. At night, a series of lights will be used in place of storm flags denoting the same dangers. At night a red light above a white light indicates a small-craft advisory, while one light over one red light means a gale warning. And for stronger storms, namely tropical storms and hurricanes, two red lights are used in a particular combination. For tropical storms, one red light over another indicates a tropical storm, while hurricane warnings are symbolized by the display of two red lights with a single white light between them is a hurricane warning.

Even without the advantages of electronic communications or displayed indicators of an approaching hurricane/tropical cyclone, there are notable changes in the weather than one can take notice of that points to the arrival of these tropical storms—despite the fact that in many cases, the warning signs that a hurricane is approaching are not apparent until a hurricane has gotten close to making landfall. As a hurricane approaches, there will be a notable increase in the size and frequency of ocean waves as they sweep ashore (i.e., the periods between waves will begin to decrease). Eventually, chop and whitecaps (rough waves and crested foam) will begin to overtake the surface of the water, leading to increasingly rough seas. Ocean swell may increase to about 6 feet (1.8 m.) in height. Waves will hit the shore about every nine seconds.

The air pressure will begin to fall steadily about 36 hours prior to a hurricane's landfall. If there is a barometer nearby, readings will indicate this notable drop in the measurable air pressure as the storm approaches. As the moves to approximately 30 hours out from landfall, the air pressure will begin to plummet. While some believe a drop in barometric pressure can aggravate arthritis or lead to headaches, the most reliable way to detect a drop in barometric pressure is by checking a barometer.

A few other signs, such as an increase in ocean swell and driving rain, can be seen 18 to 72 hours before the main part of a hurricane begins to approach. The rain may become more wind-driven and steady, falling more at an angle than directly vertical from the sky. This change in weather may be signaling the approach of the hurricane's outermost rainbands. At this point, the oncoming storm may be less than 24 hours from landfall, in which instance the rainfall will only become more heavy and wind-driven. The rain will become into a continual downpour around 6 hours before a hurricane makes landfall, resulting in some flooding in low-lying areas.

Finally, wind speed will increase as a hurricane gets closer to making landfall, from around 11 mph 36 hours before landfall to as high as 104 mph one hour before landfall. Unsecured and loose objects will begin to blow about, and tree branches will begin to fall, break, and eventually snap off in the face of increasing wind speeds.

Those who live in areas where hurricanes/tropical cyclones are likely to occur, particularly those who live in coastal regions and/or adjacent land regions should become more vigilant during the time of year when these storms are known to form (i.e., the various "hurricane seasons" for the appropriate ocean regions around the world). In the U.S., this would be the period between is June 1st through Nov. 30th in the Atlantic and May 15th through Nov. 30th in the Eastern Pacific region. Between the warnings of meteorologists, electronic communications of storm watches and warnings, and increased personal vigilance, potential injuries and/or deaths from hurricanes should be kept to a minimum for most vulnerable regions.

The No-Nonsense Guide To Hurricane Safety

How to Prepare In The Event Of A Hurricane...

The best way to prepare for a hurricane, like most other natural disasters, is to be proactive! Those who reside in hurricane-prone regions should have a prepared plan of action in the event of a hurricane-related emergency. In planning for the threat of a hurricane (or tropical storm), every course of action related to an emergency plan should be based on advanced preparation of the anticipated disruptions that are sure to come if a major hurricane makes landfall in the region where people reside.

Understand your hurricane risk

When making contingency plans for a possible hurricane/tropical cyclone, the level of preparedness should be in proportion to the actual threat potential for these storms to strike a given area. Those who should be most concerned about a hurricane or tropical storm threat are those who live along coastal regions or on islands located on ocean waters where these storms have a history of making landfall. In the U.S. and its territories, these areas include states bordering the Gulf Coast (i.e., the Gulf of Mexico) and the Atlantic Ocean, and in the waters of the central and Western Pacific Oceans (where a few U.S., territories are). In addition, those living in adjacent inland areas are just as at risk from tropical storms and depressions from downgraded hurricanes that track inward from the coastline after initial landfall.

The map below conveys the ocean and adjacent land regions (including North America and the United States) around the globe where tropical cyclones occur, and how the related frequency rate for these regions.

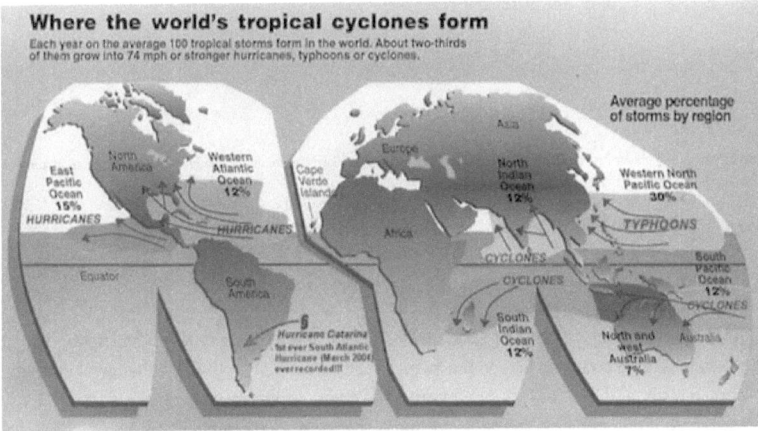

Build/Purchase A Hurricane Emergency Kit

In the event of a disaster such as a hurricane, emergency first-responders might have a difficult time reaching those affected. In worst-case scenarios, a major hurricane or strong tropical storm can be expected to disrupt basic municipal-provided accommodations such as electricity and businesses can be expected to be disrupted, perhaps for extended periods of time. The best way to confront the possibility of such disruptions is by planning to have a "disaster kit" handy just in case.

A disaster kit is a collection of supplies and basic items which might be needed in the event of a hurricane, the purpose of which is to assist in survival until either the crisis has passed, or until help arrives. These kits can be purchased either online or in some brick-and-mortar stores, prepackaged with most anticipated essentials. The prices of these prepackaged disaster kits will vary, depending on how stocked they are with supplies. Some pre-packaged kits contain basic supplies such as first aid kits, bottled water, and flashlights. The more expensive deluxe kits might include extra amenities such as a small portable toilet and/or water purification tablets in the event that the water supply is disrupted. Disaster kits can just as easily be created by purchasing anticipated items individually, collecting and storing them in the event that they are needed. Once purchased or gathered together, emergency items should be stored in a container of some type, such as a moderate-sized plastic tote or foot locker capable of being sealed or closed for protection. This also allows for the kit to be easily transported in the event that evacuations are ordered.

An example of the type of plastic tote (with a sealed lid) which can be used to store a tornado disaster kit. A footlocker of approximately the same size would be just as effective a storage location.

At the very least, an effective disaster kit should include the following:

Clothing & Bedding:

- An extra change of clothing for every person anticipated to take cover in the shelter is a reasonable precaution to take in the face of such a possibility. An extra change of clothing should include both underwear and foot in the event of maximum need.
- Waterproof rain ponchos, in the event that a change of clothing might not be practical. Rain ponchos serve the same purpose as an extra change of clothing, especially considering that weather often remains **inclement after the hurricane has passed.**
- Several blankets, preferably one for every person anticipated to evacuate to one of the established designated storm shelters. Blankets can be folded into impromptu padded sleeping surfaces in the case of extended need. For the extra expense sleeping bags can be purchased in

lieu of blankets, however, blankets are more practical and can be utilized for more multiple purposes in the event of an emergency.

- Two pairs of sturdy work or safety gloves. Oftentimes, scattered debris and other structural pilings end up strewn across large swaths of an affected area in the aftermath of a hurricane. In removing these obstructions, a sturdy pair of gloves would protect the hands from sharp edges and other potentially dangerous objects while moving trying to evacuate from damaged structures.

Foodstuffs:

- Although in many cases government and charitable resources such as the Federal Emergency Management Agency (FEMA), the Red Cross, or church-based charities can be expected to provide relief in the form of food and other necessities, this may always be immediately so. A 2-3 day supply of non-perishable, no refrigeration-required food should be packed away somewhere inside or near the shelter itself in the event of loss of power. Additionally, the foods selected for storage should be of the type that are tightly sealed, and requires very little or no preparation (i.e., cooking) and/or need for water. Ideally, food products with similarly close expiration dates should be purchased and stored together, so as to make replacing them at the same time easier if they expire before use.

  If storage space availability is limited, consider purchasing military-style Meals Ready to Eat (MRE) packet from surplus or camping stores. MREs are small packets of food rations that require just a little water or maybe some heat to prepare. And in the case of individuals who feel that they *must* have heat-prepared food, consider packing away "canned heat." Canned heat is a concentrated source of cooking heat which is designed to be burned directly from its canned casing as an emergency source of heat for the limited cooking of food (it can be found in most camping stores). For foods that don't require cooking, keep track of their individual expiration dates.
- Canned meats such as tuna and beef (jerky) have extended storage lives, so such items should be a main staple of any stored food (unless there are vegetarians present, in which case canned vegetables should be included).
- High energy food sources such as protein, energy, and/or granola bars are idea for storage. They require less space than canned foods, even those that don't require preparation.
- Bottled water. Stored in sealed plastic bottles, bottle water keeps amazingly well for extended periods. The U.S. Food and Drug Administration (FDA) estimates that most bottled water has a potentially indefinite shelf life, so replacing drinking water to maintain its availability in case of emergency use should not be a major concern. Ideally, one gallon of water per person, per day should be stored for emergencies. However, Nursing and/or pregnant women, children, and individuals with pre-existing medical conditions might need more water.
- Canned juices, milk, and/or soup (milk and soup can be purchased in powered form, and as such tend to have long shelf lives. Extra water should be considered if powdered foods are going to be used).

- Crackers, cookies, and other ready-to-eat snack foods add variety as well as supplement the food supply.

Supplies/Communication:

- Waterproof matches, lighters, and/or candles (preferably those that come contained in a semi-enclosed glass holder to prevent the flame from being extinguished) for a source of light in the event of the loss of power. Alternatives to flame-based illumination to consider (in the event that gas leaks from exposed or damaged gas lines might create an explosive hazard) include a rechargeable flashlight or penlight, or long-period glow sticks
- A battery-powered radio for keeping updated on vital information or instructions. A better alternative might be to consider purchasing one of the types of portable radios that rely on neither batteries nor electricity. These units are powered by cranking a handle, which charges a miniature generator inside the unit enough to power it *without* batteries or electricity for a limited amount of time.
- An all-purpose toolkit, or a multi-tool such as a heavy-duty Swiss army knife or Weatherman multi-purpose instrument. Tools and other such implements can be invaluable in the event that there is a need to clear debris and other obstructions from areas of protection and blocked evacuation paths leading from shelters.
- A non-electric/hand-powered can-opener (if not a function of a multi-purpose tool).
- A pack of batteries, preferably an assorted pack containing multiple sizes for battery-powered instruments (e.g., radio).
- Plastic utensils, paper plates, and/or Tupperware or plastic containers (with lids) for serving food.
- Sanitation supplies, in the event that any assistance is not immediate and facilities are not immediately available. A stock of sanitation supplies that includes toilet paper/towelettes, liquid bottled soap or detergent, a 5-gallon bucket with a lid, plastic garbage bags with ties, a disinfectant, a strong cleaner such as bleach, and personal hygiene items should be sufficient to lessen the hardships of extended periods without access to facilities.
- A first-aid kit. First-aid kits of varying degrees of items can be purchased at mostly any "big box" store, or can be created from scratch based on anticipated needs. At the very least, an effective first-aid kit should contain bandages (the plastic adhesive, rolled cloth, and/or the "liquid" varieties), roller cloth bandages, sterile gauze pads, towelette wipes, medical tape, a liquid antiseptic (e.g., alcohol and/or peroxide), anti-bacterial soap, smelling salts, petroleum jelly, latex gloves, tweezers, scissors, a thermometer, and aspirin or some other pain-reliever.
- A small, portable electric generator, in the event that electrical power is lost due to downed electrical wires

Create an Emergency Plan

Because tropical storm systems like hurricanes vary in strength, intensity, and duration, the individual level of danger presented by them can vary as well. Any hurricane is potentially dangerous and/or deadly. As such, all hurricanes merit the respect—and in some cases, the necessity—of creating personal contingency planning in order to avoid injuries and loss of life which could result from any level category of these storms. The urgency of the weather advisory issued is the best criteria by which enacting such plans should be considered. Weather *watches and warnings* should be the basis for putting plans and procedures into action

During a hurricane watch, the following preparations should be followed:

- Local television/radio news stations should be monitored for weather-related updates. In addition, NOAA/weather radios should turned on and likewise monitored for weather advisories.
- **Plan for darkness. In most hurricanes,** electrical power will likely be lost. An electrical generator, extra water, batteries, and portable sources of light will become necessities.
- Existing evacuation plans should be reviewed (most local hurricane-prone municipalities in the U.S. not only have evacuation plans in the event of an approaching hurricane, but have designated shelters where individuals are invited to reside until the danger of the storm passes
- Evacuation kits and/or family disaster supplies kits should be checked and moved to an areas of easy access in the event of an evacuation. Any additional and necessary items that should also be gathered for use during a hurricane emergency.
- Family members should be contacted in order to coordinate storm preparations and to be made aware of emergency plans. This includes relatives/acquaintances who (preferably) reside outside of the emergency/storm area(s).
- Important documents and photos should be placed in either waterproof bags or containers and carried in the event of an evacuation. It is also a good idea to keep extra money (i.e., cash) on hand in the event that cash dispersal machines (i.e., ATMs) become non-functional or banks close due to a lack of electrical power.
- Food storage units (refrigerators/freezers/coolers) should be turned to their coldest settings to extend the preservation of foodstuffs in the event that electricity is lost during storms. These units should then only be opened when necessary and close quickly afterwards.
- An ample supply of bottled water should be purchased in advance of any (possible) deteriorating weather conditions that might prevent buying later. Additional water should be frozen in cartons or plastic jugs. Finally, other containers should be filled with clean water for later use (such as for scrubbing/personal cleansing, and brushing teeth).
- Bathtubs should be scrubbed and filled with extra water; keep bucket handy for flushing toilets.
- Vehicles should be fully fuelled in the event that evacuation is ordered (do not attempt travel an evacuation route on less than a full tank). Propane tanks and generators should also be fueled.
- Cover all of your home's windows. Permanent storm shutters offer the best protection for windows. The best alternative option is to board up windows plywood, cut to fit and ready to be secured with nails. Contrary to popular belief, taping windows offers little or no protection from their breaking.
- All loose objects such as outdoor furniture, trash cans, yard figurines, and grills that are usually found outside of homes should be either anchored or stored indoors until the storm threat passes; such loose objects can become dangerous flying projectiles in a major hurricane (or

even tropical storm).
- All boats should be moored (tied down).
- Secure outdoor gates
- All garage doors, gates, and other loose points of entry should be secured with strong rope or by some other means.
- Trees should be trimmed to make them more wind-resistant, as well as lessen the incident of falling branches, which could injure or even kill those they fall on.
- Individual residing in mobile homes should ensured that such relatively weak dwellings are tied down/anchored before leaving and taking shelter elsewhere. Mobile homes are some of the most dangerous places to be during a storm on the order of a hurricane because they can so easily blown apart by the storm's sustained winds.
- If individuals find themselves in a high-rise building during a watch, they should consider taking shelter on the lower floors.

It should noted that although when a hurricane watch may be issued, it doesn't necessarily mean that the watch area will sustain a direct hit from the main portion of a hurricane. Hurricane watches tend to be issued for a wide swath of area along the tracking path of an approaching storm. This is because forecasting tracking models are based on a measure of statistical probabilities, and that there remains a significant level of uncertainty as to where a hurricane's actual path may force it to make actual landfall. Meteorologists call this area of general uncertainty (but to where a hurricane's landfall is statistically probable) the "cone of uncertainty."

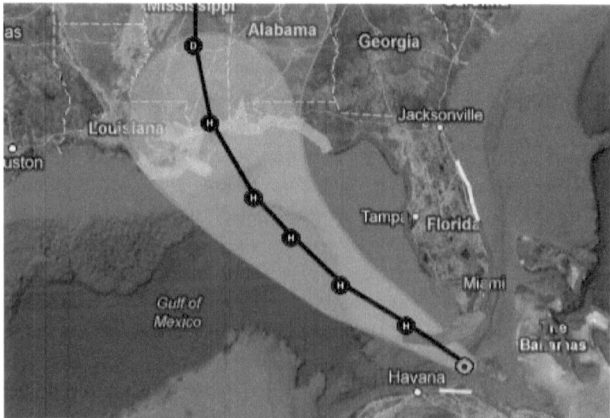

An example of the "cone of uncertainty" for Tropical Storm Issac's (2012) path as it makes an approach toward the U.S. Gulf Coast region—with the probability of it strengthening to a full-fledged hurricane by the time of its expected landfall. The purple colors indicate the areas where hurricane watches were issued; blue areas indicate tropical storm watches (red indicates tropical storm warnings).

However, because of this level of uncertainty when it comes to hurricane forecasting, those who find themselves in a watch area should take the suggested precautions. It is usually certain that those living within the cone of uncertainty will experience, at the very least, strong tropical storm level winds and conditions.

During a hurricane warning, individuals should (in addition to the suggested courses of action for a hurricane watch:

- **Heed evacuation warnings!** A mandatory evacuation order issued by local or state authorities means that those residing in the affected area *must leave* when told to do so. This is especially true for residents living in a manufactured or mobile home. Residents in low-lying areas and on barrier islands may be required to evacuate depending upon the storm's projected path and flooding/storm surge potential. Even if an evacuation order is not issued, strong consideration should be given to doing so anyway. Even if the affected area is not directly impacted by a hurricane, tropical storm-force winds can topple a lightly-constructed structures like mobile homes. Dwellings of comparatively equal weak construction design are also ill-advised places to seek shelter (such as a garage or a buildings with large uninterrupted interior space and but weak roof support). The best kind of dwelling to take shelter is one made up of sturdy construction, such as a school, municipal government office building, or other reinforced structure; buildings constructed of concrete provide the best protection from the elements in a hurricane
- Relatives and/or acquaintances should be notified that an evacuation is underway, and informed as to where/what particular shelter to contact.
- Any prepared evacuation/disaster kits should be loaded for travel, along with any important Documents (drivers licenses, insurance papers, property deeds, photos, address book/family contacts, etc.).
- If arrangements have been made for pets to be boarded, they should be taken to any prearranged pet shelter (most animal care facilities will accept pets within 24 hours of a hurricane's landfall). Some shelters will allow pets to be boarded with their owners (such information should be known ahead of time). However, pets are not allowed at Red Cross shelters – only official service animals.
- The residence to be evacuated should be locked up and vacated. Extended periods of travel time should be allotted for (factored in). Consider for allowing at least twice the usual travel time as travel is made toward the predetermined emergency shelter or host residence.

Plan Your Shelter

In most hurricane-prone regions, both local and state/provincial authorities tend to have contingency plans to ensure the safety of those residing in these areas in the event of an actual hurricane. Most of these plans involve ordering evacuations from areas threatened with being directly impacted by the initial landfall area of an approaching storm. In many coastal areas, designated evacuation routes have been established to help expedite thus process. In some high-density coastal areas, normally two-directional highways can be changed—by virtue of emergency orders—to accommodate single-directional traffic to further expedite the evacuation process.

In addition to evacuations, local municipal contingency plans tend to involve establishing and/or designating shelters where, in the event of a hurricane/tropical cyclone. Those ordered to leave should evacuate to the assigned and/or designated shelter as soon as possible. Information about bringing pets along, the exact location of local shelters, travel time, and other pertinent information should be gathered beforehand, as to help lessen the chance for panic should an evacuation becomes necessary. In minimum-level hurricanes, tropical storms, or in instances where residents have limited resources, individuals may only be *advised* (as opposed to *ordered*) to evacuate), where leaving is optional. In such cases where individuals are resigned to remain in their homes should (in addition to the prescribed actions under a hurricane watch):

- Windows should be covered with either storm shutters or plywood securely nailed (at this point, any needed materials used to secure property should have already been purchased).
- Continue to monitor radios and television news broadcasts for emergency information (its advised to have an ample supply of batteries to power such devices in the event that electrical power is lost during the storm. An alternative (and better) option is to monitor news and weather reports over hand cranked radios/televisions.
- Vehicles should be moved into an interior shelter such as a garage or carport. Parking underneath trees and utility poles should be avoided.
- Ensure that an ample supply of clean clothes is available in the event that power is disrupted.
- Flashlight, radio, television, and cell phone batteries should be stored in an easily assessable location. Rechargeable batteries should be charged to full capacity for immediate use.

An alternative to evacuating to an emergency shelter or an out-of-town relative is to build a *safe room*, similar to those found in regions where tornadoes regularly occur. A **safe room** is essentially a windowless box (i.e., enclosed and isolated room), usually located inside a house or other dwelling where families can take shelter to escape the danger of wind-borne projectiles during a hurricane (or tornadoes). A safe room prepared in anticipation of a hurricane should be where the emergency disaster kit is housed when not in use. At the very least, a hurricane safe room should be stocked with items like bottled water, non-perishable food, blankets, battery-operated lights, a radio and a first-aid kit. Hurricane can take hours to pass through (unlike tornadoes, which blow through an area comparatively quickly), and it may be necessary to prepare for an extended stay inside a safe room until the storm passes.

The major disadvantage of a hurricane safe room is that they are not air-tight. As such, they also tend not to be water-tight. Given the potential for storm surge and flooding in a hurricane, safe rooms can become drowning hazards under such circumstances. The best way to avoid this potential scenario is to consider the flood threat for the area where a hurricane safe room will be installed (most insurance companies have access to information regarding the flood risks for a given area).

In the event that no evacuation order or the decision is made to remain in the home during the hurricane, remain calm. The loud and intimidating nature of the high winds, the torrential and driving rains, and the threat of tornadoes can make riding out a hurricane an often terrifying ordeal. To minimize the danger or the risk to personal harm, consider the following guidelines:

- Remain indoors during the storm; avoid the impulse to go outside to observe. Avoid glass doors and windows, even if they are boarded/shuttered. The safest place to be is an interior room, a closet or bathroom on the lowest level of the home.
- At some point, the eye of the storm may pass over the affected area. At this point, there will be

a short period of calm. However, it should be remembered that once the eye passes, the wind speeds will both rapidly increase and change direction (i.e., hurricane force winds and will blow from the opposite direction).

- Electricity should be disconnected (at the circuit panel) if flooding becomes a threat. Avoid the use of electrical appliances and equipment. Major appliances such as the air conditioner and water heaters should be turned off to reduce damage if power is lost during the storm. Since lightning is a major threat during most hurricanes, maintain distance from electrical equipment. Avoid the use of landline telephones, or showering during the storm.

An important point of note when opting to remain at home during a hurricane is to consider the availability of emergency services during the height of the storm. If an evacuation order is given by authorities and subsequently ignored, authorities will often issue warning to those opting to stay behind that emergency response personnel will not be dispatched in a potential emergency or rescue situation. Furthermore, in some cases authorities will often ask those opting to not to evacuate to supply contact information on their "next of kin" (i.e., closest living relative). The reason for this is so that in the event that death (or a major injury) results from of the decision to remain at home during a hurricane, the authorities are able to demonstrate no responsibility in any such negative consequence, as well as making identifying the body of any deceased easier (if the individual remaining lives alone). This worse-case scenario was the case with many who perished in New Orleans during 2005's Hurricane Katrina. To avoid this possibility, it is highly advised that any evacuation order be followed without unnecessary delay.

What to Avoid

Just as there are precautions that one can take to limit the potential for injury and death in the event of a hurricane, there are actions and decisions that one can make which may put one more in jeopardy, thus increasing risk to life and limb. Whether the decision is made to evacuate or "ride out the storm" at home, there are practices which should be heeded to stave off the risk of injury and/or death. Among the things to avoid before, during, and after a hurricane are:

- Falls. Be aware that falls caused indirectly by the effects of a hurricane while initiating preventive measures or cleaning up are a potential hazard. Before and after hurricanes, deaths and injuries have occurred as a result of people falling from roofs (while attempting to make repairs), ladders (as they cover up exposed windows), and trees (as they attempt to cut dangling branches).
- Being struck by falling objects. Dangling tree branches, signs or siding are always a present danger both before and after a storm. Often, the strong precursor-winds that begin before the arrival of the strongest part of a hurricane can be just as (potentially) dangerous in creating falling object hazards. Always be aware of their potential presence.
- Punctures & cuts. After a hurricane, debris is often strewn across large areas. Much of this debris may contain both sharp edges created as they were ripped by a hurricane's winds (such as metal street and building signs) and nails. In addition, there is usually the danger of broken glass from unsecured windows. In the area of hurricane impact, one should be aware of

his/her surroundings at all times. If possible, boots and gloves should be worn in areas of such damage, especially is engaging in cleaning and debris removal activities.

- Electrocution. Both hurricane and tropical storm-force winds will cause power lines and utility poles to snap. The resulting downed wires might contain live electrical currents; electrical sparking is the surest sign of this (although this may not be present in every circumstance). The most dangerous scenario involving this danger is when live broken wires come into contact with water (such as flood waters, which often hide fallen electrical wires). This conducts lethal amounts of electrical current away from the immediate vicinity of the wire itself. Many times as a result of these instances in the aftermath of a hurricane, individuals have lost their lives by coming into contact with live electrical wires. Keep distant from downed wires, especially if the smell of an electrical fire is in the air. If possible, keep clear of flood waters. Ensure all appliances are dry and free of water before plugging them into an outlet.

- Asphyxiation. Although such a threat seems out of place in discussing the dangers of a hurricane, many people have died from suffocating on dangerous fumes caused by the attempt to supply electricity to their homes by way of a gas-powered generator. When these generators are operated and left unattended in enclosed locations (like a garage, of an unoccupied room indoors), deadly carbon monoxide fumes can quickly accumulate. The result can be carbon monoxide poisoning, a buildup of these oxygen-supplanting fumes in the bloodstream. These fumes are deadly if allowed to build up in unventilated enclosed areas. Those sleeping under such conditions are especially vulnerable to this threat (many who have died from carbon monoxide poisoning did so while sleeping). In 2011's Hurricane Ike (which made landfall in Texas), some 13 people died from carbon monoxide poisoning, mostly as a result of the improper use of electrical generators. Generators should be operated outdoors, in a semi-sheltered area that provides for ample ventilation.

- Drowning. Between the threat of storm surges and flooding, drownings are the chief cause of deaths in hurricanes/tropical typhoons. In addition to the lives accidentally lost to drowning, others have been lost due to questionable decisions made during the most inclimate conditions during these storms. Some of those who chose to engage in recreational activities such as surfing and swimming during the high ocean swells created by these storms have perished, ignoring the danger inherent in such activities such threatening conditions. In other cases, people have attempted to drive through flood waters in the midst of hurricane conditions, not realizing—until it's too late—that a great deal of flood deaths have resulted from unsuccessfully doing so. Remaining indoors in a place/shelter of relative safety during a hurricane or tropical storm conditions is the best way to avoid death by drowning. Evacuating from endangered coastal areas when told to do so is an even better policy to observe. Lastly, never attempt to drive through flood waters—even water that appears to be shallow. It takes less than 2 feet of moving water (0.60 meters) to float most vehicles.

- Fire. During the loss of power that occurs in the aftermath of a hurricane, its normal for those without electricity to attempt to light candles in order to find their way around in the resulting dark. However, unattended and/or misused candles and other sources of flame (such as flame-based lanterns) can result in fires that quickly get out of control. Flame-based sources of light should be monitored at all times; never unattended. In possible, glass covers (ironically, called "hurricanes") should be used to shelter open flames on candles. Never use candles or open flames in high winds If possible, battery-powered sources of light should be used instead. Additionally, gas camp stoves and portable grills should only be used outdoors, away from flammable materials.
- Food poisoning. Food of questionable edibility should be avoided. Food can be kept in an unopened refrigerator for up to 24 hours in the absence of electricity—longer if frozen. If food begins to smell badly or if there is some doubt as to whether it is safe to eat, avoid eating it and simply throw it out. If possible, use canned food and water stored in food-safe containers. To further avoid any poisoning threat, all other water should be boiled before drinking.
- Stubbornness. Avoid mindsets that run counter to the request of authorities. Heed the requests of emergency (management) and rescue personnel. Roads may be blocked, flooding may be widespread and tap water may be unsafe to drink. Use radios and televisions to follow the advice, suggestions, and orders of emergency workers, and follow directions.

After A Hurricane

The good news regarding hurricanes is that, thanks to modern forecasting advances, many potential deaths and injuries can be avoided as people learn these storms can avoided by flowing instructions to evacuate when the of landfall arises. The bad news is that despite this reality, people continue to be injured and even killed by these storms globally every year—and that includes the U.S. Another negative point about hurricanes is that they tend to affect moderately large areas, and many people. Some individuals may lose everything they own, while others may have to contend with an extended period without modern conveniences such as electricity and internet connections. Some might have had their homes blown away by powerful winds, while others may be forced to absorb the loss of property that is underwater; all in the storm area will be impacted on some level.

In the aftermath of a hurricane, it is important to remain indoors at home, or within the protected confines of an emergency shelter until the "all clear" is given by authorities, and it is deemed safe to leave. In the event that it was necessary to evacuate an affected community, it is equally important to avoid returning until authorities have determined that it is safe to return. In the meantime, keeping clear of disaster areas is highly recommended (unless local authorities request volunteers). It's advised that family members should remain together during this period as a source of mutual emotional support (be cognizant of any exhibited symptoms of stress and fatigue within the family).

Those affected may want to continue to monitor local radio and television newscasts. In most cases, these will be the primary means by which important information and instructions will be disseminated by local officials. Broadcasts could contain vital information about securing medical as well as how to apply financial (government) assistance if needed.

Depending on where and under what circumstances shelter was sought, there may be injuries to those who sought shelter at home, or in emergency shelter. If so, and depending on the type and severity of injuries, it will be imperative to secure medical assistance. If available, a first-aid kit (preferably one is available in a disaster/emergency kit) may be used to stabilize or address any minor wounds before seeking further assistance (on the assumption that the injuries aren't *too* severe). In many instances, injuries occur after a hurricane/typhoon has passed—many happening during rescue attempts, cleanup, and other post-hurricane activities (see the section, "What to Avoid").

When driving from designated shelters or returning home (if allowed by authorities), drive *only* if it is safe and/or necessary. Not only will streets and roadways likely be filled with debris, but in some cases, roadways can be damaged or weakened by flood waters. The result can be the collapse of roads under the weight of an automobile. In some instances, hurricanes have caused entire streets and bridges to be washed away by resulting floodwaters and storm surges, stranding those seeking to leave devastated areas or keeping others from returning home. Travelling (or walking) near rivers and streams should be avoided until any present flood threat has passed.

Because hurricanes and tropical storms often damage power lines, gas lines, or electrical systems, there is a risk of fire, electrocution, or an explosion so caution should be employed when entering any or exiting structure that has been damaged. Do not touch downed power lines or objects in contact with downed lines. Report any electrical hazards to the police, the fire department, or to a public utility or other emergency worker. If possible, wear sturdy footwear, long sleeves, and gloves when handling or walking on or near debris.

Finally, property owners, renters, and businesses affected by hurricane damage should contact their insurance companies and/or the appropriate insurance agents. Insurance personnel should be given as complete a list as possible of any items damaged or destroyed by the storm. Items damaged should not be disposed of until insurance adjusters have had a chance to view them. Adjusters will also need to inspect property for a specific cause of damage.[7] For homeowners without insurance, contact the local Red Cross of the FEMA Disaster Recovery Center for assistance.

---

[7] In flood-prone regions and low-lying areas, most insurance companies will make a distinction between the exact causes of property damage after a hurricane in order to determine whether a homeowner qualifies for compensation of losses. Water damage and losses linked to flooding will likely be determined to be ineligible for loss compensation because, in most cases, only specified flood insurance can cover such

Summary

Unlike most other natural disasters, hurricanes/tropical cyclones do not "just happen." They form out over the ocean over a period of time, and may ride existing wind and weather patterns toward the coastlines of land areas where population centers are located. Those who might find themselves in the paths of these storms are typically given enough warnings in advanced of any landfall to avoid being endangered. However, despite all of the technological and communications advantages that help those who might be affected by a hurricane avoid becoming victims of these storms, hurricanes kill (and injure) more than any other type of storm worldwide. Every year, and depending on where a hurricane/tropical typhoon strikes, hundreds or even thousands of people can die as a result of these storms.[8] In most cases, if consideration and effort were put into making effective preparations prior to hurricane/typhoon threats, injuries and deaths could easily be avoided.

In addition to heeding advanced warnings and creating—an enacting—an emergency plan to mitigate the threat posed by hurricanes, the necessity of vigilance is also a factor in reducing the potential for injuries and/or deaths. Depending on where one lives on land adjacent to the 7 known hurricane-spawning ocean regions, being aware of the start of hurricane season and any of any weather-related activities ongoing in the ocean during this period can potentially create even *more* advanced warning of a potential hurricane threat.

Lastly, hurricanes present a constant level of threat prior to, during, and even after landfall. Between the initial deteriorating weather conditions, the high winds, torrential rains, storm surges, flooding, and the hazards created by devastated population centers (i.e., dangerous debris), hurricanes represent a major disruption to the lives of those impacted. But at every level, following common sense, avoiding questionable decisions, and making the proper preparations can mitigate these threats to life and limb.

---

losses—and flood protection is normally not written into most homeowners and property insurance policies. Flood insurance must be purchased as a separate policy. However, damage and losses as a direct result of wind damage will usually be compensated. In a few extreme cases, homeowners-insurance company disagreements over such interpretations of damage causes can result in litigation.

[8] The figures for typhoon/hurricane deaths globally vary, based on the size, strength, and duration of a particular storm, where it makes landfall, the level of advanced warning provided to threatened populations, infrastructure of the affected areas, and other variables. Typhoon Nina, which struck areas of China in August of 1975 resulted in 100,000. By comparison, Hurricane Katrina in 2005 which struck the Gulf Coast of the U.S., killed over 1,800 (although the official death toll will never be fully known).

Notes

Hurricane/Typhoon History

Date	Location	Impact/Significance
September 8, 1900	Galveston (Island), Texas	The 1900 hurricane was the deadliest weather disaster in United States history. Storm tides of 8 to 15 ft inundated the whole of Galveston Island, as well as other portions of the nearby Texas coast. These tides were largely responsible for the 8,000 deaths (with estimates ranging from 6,000 to 12,000)
November 12, 1970	Bengal Coast region, East Pakistan	The deadliest tropical cyclone in recorded history, the so-called "Bhola Cyclone" of 1970 killed between 150,000 and 500,000 people.
October 1998	Honduras, El Salvador, Nicaragua, Central, Guatemala America	Hurricane Mitch was a slow-moving tropical storm that virtually stalled over a region of Central America, causing some 11,000 deaths (with another several thousand missing and presumed dead). The storm caused a 2-day rain event resulted in some 4 inches (10 centimeters) of precipitation that triggered deadly mudslides and flooding—making it the 2nd deadliest hurricane on record.
August-September 2005	New Orleans/Coastal regions of Louisiana, Mississippi, Alabama, Florida	Initially affecting areas of the state of Florida, Hurricane Katrina re-entered the warm waters of the Gulf of Mexico (strengthening to a category 5 storm). Katrina later made 2nd landfall (as a category 3 storm) along the U.S. Gulf Coast. It not only caused devastating and deadly storm surges, but directly contributed to the destruction of the weakly-constructed system of levees and floodwalls that were designed to protect the low-lying city of New Orleans, causing a deadly flood that added to the death toll. Katrina resulted in over 1,800 lives lost, with several hundred missing. It was the

		costliest natural disaster in U.S. history.

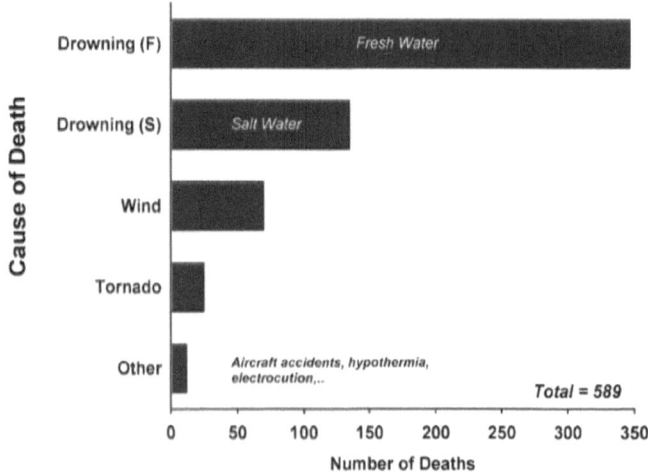

Glossary of Hurricane-Related Terms

Cyclone – is an area of intense closed-circulation rotation of winds, rains, and clouds within an atmospheric weather disturbance. In the Northern Hemisphere, cyclones rotate counter-clockwise, wise rotating clockwise in the Southern Hemisphere.

Extratropical Cyclone/Storm – is a cyclone or storm of which the primary source energy which sustains it derives from source is temperature contrasts between warm and cold air masses, rather than the warmth of tropical conditions (such as warm ocean waters).

Eye - the roughly circular area of comparative atmospheric "calm" usually found within the center of a tropical cyclone. The "eye" is characterized by light winds and the presences of few—if any—clouds within this region of the storm. The eye is either completely or partially surrounded by the eyewall cloud.

Eyewall (cloud) – is an organized band or ring of cumulonimbus clouds that surround the" eye" of a tropical cyclone/hurricane (the region of light-wind and relative atmospheric "calm" at center of a tropical storm).

Hurricane Season – is a period within the calendar year when the climatic conditions become more favorable for an increased incidence of hurricanes/tropical cyclones. The hurricane season in the Atlantic, Caribbean, and Gulf of Mexico runs from June 1 to November 30. The hurricane season in the Eastern Pacific basin runs from May 15 to November 30. The hurricane season in the Central Pacific (Asia) runs from June 1 to November 30.

Hurricane Warning – is a statement and/or weather advisory issued by government agencies responsible for monitoring (changes in) the weather and conducting weather research. A hurricane warning will be issued when conditions indicate that a tropical weather disturbance adopts characteristics that include the presence of sustained winds of at least 74 mph (119 km/h), heavy winds, and high tidal surges. This specific type of weather advisory is issued when such conditions are expected to affect specified region, usually adjacent to ocean coastlines (indicating that they are association with a tropical, subtropical, or post-tropical cyclone). Hurricane warnings are typically issued some 36 prior to the anticipated arrival of the outermost portion of a tropical cyclone/hurricane (partly because hurricane preparedness activities become difficult once winds reach tropical storm force).

Hurricane Watch – is a statement and/or weather advisory issued by government agencies responsible for monitoring (changes in) the weather and conducting weather research. A hurricane watch will be issued when conditions indicate that a tropical weather disturbance of a hurricane-level magnitude is possible for a specified region or area. Hurricane watches are typically issued some 48 hours prior to the anticipated arrival of tropical storm force winds (winds of at least 39 mph or 63 km/h), which allows for those who might be affected to initiate any storm preparations procedures (such as evacuation).

Jet Streams – are the narrow bands of strong, high-speed air currents located several miles/kilometers above the surface of the earth, in the atmosphere. These air currents are located at various latitudes, and vary in location, as affected by the rotation of the earth as well as other external forces. Jet streams often control aspects of the weather closer to the earth's surface, such as the particular track that hurricanes take as they approach landfall.

Landfall – refers to both the geographical point as well as moment in time at which a hurricane/tropical cyclone encounters the coastline after tracking across the open waters.

Rainbands - are dense bands of heavy-precipitation-producing thunderstorms that range in width from a few miles/kilometers to tens of miles/kilometers, and can be anywhere from a 50 to 300 miles (80 to 482 km) long. They are the product of maturing (or matured) tropical storm systems such as hurricanes, as their cloud structures become more active.

Storm Surge – is an abnormal rise in sea levels, usually accompanying a hurricane or other tropical storm system. A storm surge is estimated by difference in the known height of a water/ocean level at normal levels (i.e., in the absence of a storm or at astronomical high-tide), and that the observable level of said water/ocean base in the presence of a storm.

Tropical Disturbance – is a tropical weather system characterized by an organizing and/or active cluster of ocean-based thunderstorms.

Tropical Depression - A tropical cyclone characterized by the presence of maximum sustained wind speeds of 38 mph (62 km/h) or less.

Tropical Storm - A tropical cyclone characterized by the presence maximum sustained wind speeds ranging from 39 mph (63 km/h) to 73 mph (118 km/h).

Tropical Storm Warning - is a statement and/or weather advisory issued by government agencies responsible for monitoring (changes in) the weather and conducting weather research. A tropical storm warning is issued when a tropical weather system containing sustained winds of between 39 and 73 mph (63 and 118 km/h) is either occurring or imminent (for a specified area or region within 36 hours of the issuance of the advisory).

Tropical Storm Watch - is a statement and/or weather advisory issued by government agencies responsible for monitoring (changes in) the weather and conducting weather research. A tropical storm watch is issued when a tropical weather system containing sustained winds of between 39 and 73 mph (63 and 118 km/h) is possible for a specified area or region within 48 hours of the issuance of the advisory.

Appendix A:

Federal Emergency Management Agency (FEMA) contact information by region

As an extensive government agency, FEMA administrative resources (as well as contact information) have been somewhat decentralized. This is to say that, in order to expedite any assistance to local and state governments (and to limit the potential for bureaucratic confusion), FEMA was divided into regional offices that oversee regional "zones." These *Regional Operations Offices* serve as the arms of the central agency's headquarters (located in Washington D.C.) and through which all policy, managerial, resource and administrative actions effecting coordination between headquarters are initiated.

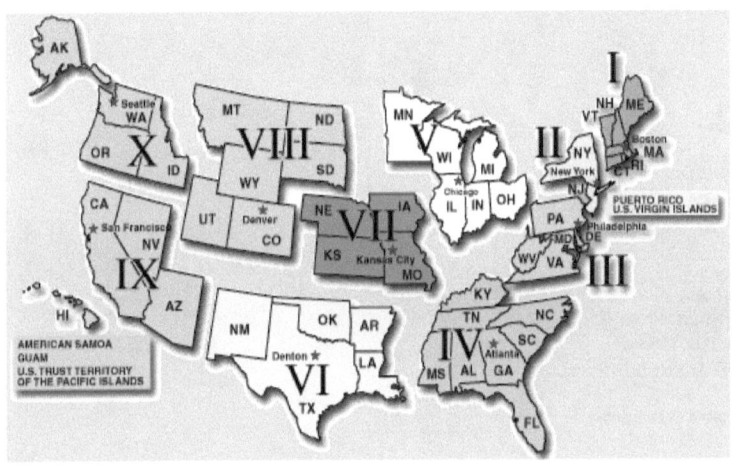

Region	Location	States Serving
Region I	Boston, MA	CT, MA, ME, NH, RI, VT
Region II	New York, NY	NJ, NY, PR, USVI
Region III	Philadelphia, PA	DC, DE, MD, PA, VA, WV
Region IV	Atlanta, GA	AL, FL, GA, KY, MS, NC, SC, TN
Region V	Chicago, IL	IL, IN, MI, MN, OH, WI

Region	Location	States Serving
Region VI	Denton, TX	AR, LA, NM, OK, TX
Region VII	Kansas City, MO	IA, KS, MO, NE
Region VIII	Denver, CO	CO, MT, ND, SD, UT, WY
Region IX	Oakland, CA	AZ, CA, HI, NV, GU, AS, CNMI, RMI, FM
Region X	Bothell, WA	AK, ID, OR, WA

Contact:

FEMA Region I
99 High St.
Boston, MA 02110
1-877-336-2734
Email

Federal Region II
26 Federal Plaza
New York, NY 10278-0002
Telephone: (212) 680-3600
FEMA-R2-ExternalAffairs@fema.dhs.gov

Puerto Rico and Virgin Islands

Mailing address:
Carribean Division
PO Box 70105
San Juan PR 00936-0105

Physical address:
New San Juan Office Bldg
159 Calle Chardon, 6th Floor
Hato Rey, PR 00918
Telephone: (787) 296-3500

FEMA Region III
One Independence Mall, 6th Floor
615 Chestnut Street
Philadelphia, PA 19106-4404
(215) 931-5500

FEMA Region IV

The No-Nonsense Guide To Hurricane Safety

Federal Emergency Management Agency
3003 Chamblee Tucker Road
Atlanta, GA 30341
Office: 770-220-5200
Fax Number: 770-220-5230

FEMA Region V
Federal Emergency Management Agency
536 South Clark Street, 6th Floor
Chicago, IL 60605
(312) 408-5500

FEMA Region VI
Federal Emergency Management Agency
FRC 800 North Loop 288
Denton, TX 76209-3698
E-Mail: FEMA-R6-RRCC-PrivateSector@fema.dhs.gov
Tribal Affairs
E-Mail Norma.Reyes@fema.dhs.gov
Telephone: 940-898-5233

FEMA Region VII or Federal Emergency Management Agency
9221 Ward Parkway, Suite 300
Kansas City, MO. 64114-3372
Telephone: (816) 283-7061
Tribal Contact
E-mail: jonathan.weinberg@fema.dhs.gov
Telephone: (816) 809-4128

FEMA Region VIII or Federal Emergency Management Agency
Federal Emergency Management Agency
Denver Federal Center
Building 710, Box 25267
Denver, CO 80225-0267
(303) 235-4800

FEMA Region IX
1111 Broadway, Oakland, CA 94607
Phone:(510) 627-7140
Pacific Area Office
(808) 851-7900
Southern California Field Office
(626) 431-3000

FEMA Region X or Federal Emergency Management Agency
Federal Regional Center
130 - 228th Street, Southwest
Bothell, WA 98021-8627
(425) 487-4600

Appendix B:

Disaster-Relief Organizations and Charities

This following is a partial list of the many disaster-relief and charitable organizations that those affected by tornado emergencies can turn to in times of need. Below is a sample of the most notable of these organizations.

American Red Cross
http://www.redcross.org/find-help

Catholic Charities USA
http://www.catholiccharitiesusa.org/what-we-do/disaster-operations/

Children's Disaster Services (Church of the Brethren)
http://www.brethren.org/cds/

Christian Disaster Response
http://cdresponse.org/

Feeding America
http://feedingamerica.org/need-help.aspx?s_src=Y14YPDGAA&s_keyword=feedingamerica&s_subsrc=feedingamerica

National Organization for Victim Assistance (NOVA)
http://www.trynova.org/

Salvation Army
http://www.salvationarmyusa.org/

Jewish federations of North America
http://www.jewishfederations.org/

The No-Nonsense Guide To Hurricane Safety

World Vision

Index

The No-Nonsense Guide To Hurricane Safety

References

Dean, Cornelia. (10 Oct 2006). "Surprises in a New Tally of Areas Vulnerable to Hurricanes." New York Times. Print.

Emanuel, Kerry. Divine Wind: The History and Science of Hurricanes. New York: Oxford University Press, 2005.

Fecht, Sarah. (7 Nov 2012). "How Hurricane Forecasting Got So Good." Popular Mechanics. Retrieved 7 July 2013.

"Hurricanes." Ready.gov website (FEMA). Retrieved 3 July 2013.

"Hurricanes." Centers for Disease Control (CDC) website. Retrieved 3 July 2013.

"Hurricane Preparedness." American Red Cross website. Retrieved 2 July 2013.

"Hurricanes —The Basics." (2005). The Disaster Handbook — National Edition Hurricanes — The Basics Institute of Food and Agricultural Sciences IFAS Publication DPR-0702, University of Florida

Hurricane Research Division, Atlantic Oceanographic and Meteorological Laboratory, NOAA website. Retrieved 2 July 2013

Main, Douglas. (25 July 2012). "20 Years After Hurricane Andrew: How Storm Forecasts Have Improved." Our Amazing Planet, on Live Science website. Retrieved 7 July 2013.

Murnane, Richard J., and Kam-biu Liu, eds. Hurricanes and Typhoons: Past, Present, and Future. New York: Columbia University Press, 2004.

National Hurricane Center, National Oceanic and Atmospheric Administration (NOAA). Retrieved 1 July 2013.

National Oceanic and Atmospheric Administration (NOAA). (2008). "Hurricane Forecasting." (2008). NOAA factsheet. Washington, DC: U.S. Government Printing Office.

National Oceanic and Atmospheric Administration (NOAA) Home Page - Hurricane Katrina. Accessed 10 June 2011. http://www.katrina.noaa.gov

Neumann, Charles J. "1.3: A Global Climatology". Global Guide to Tropical Cyclone Forecasting. Bureau of Meteorology.

"Personal Hurricane Response." (2005). The Disaster Handbook — National Edition Hurricanes — The Basics Institute of Food and Agricultural Sciences IFAS Publication DPR-0702, University of Florida

Sheets, Bob, and Jack Williams. Hurricane Watch: Forecasting the Deadliest Storms on Earth. New York: Vintage, 2001.

"The 1900 Galveston Hurricane" - TIME (Magazine).com website. Retrieved: 10 June 2013.

"Tropical Cyclone." World of Earth Science. 2003. Retrieved August 17, 2013 from Encyclopedia.com: http://www.encyclopedia.com/doc/1G2-3437800621.html

The No-Nonsense Guide To Hurricane Safety

The No-Nonsense Guide To Hurricane Safety

Page 14:
http://www.hurricanescience.org/society/impacts/stormsurge/

Page 16:
NASA/NOAA GOES Project

Page 17:
NOAA
http://www.srh.noaa.gov/mfl/?n=wilma

Page 20:
The Weather Channel.com
http://www.weather.com/encyclopedia/charts/tropical/hurricanerisk.html

Page 22:
http://en.wikipedia.org/wiki/File:KatrinaNewOrleansFlooded_edit2.jpg

Page 24:
http://www.weatherman101.com/factsaboutweather.htm

Page 25:
The National Coast Guard website.
http://greatlakes.coastguard.dodlive.mil/2013/02/understanding-the-weather-can-save-the-day/

Page 27:
Illustration Credit: Jack Williams, USA Today: The Weather Book (1992)

Page 32:
http://uptownmessenger.com/2012/08/issacs-uncertain-path-prompts-hurricane-watch-for-new-orleans-area/

Page 37:
Wikipedia Images
http://commons.wikimedia.org/wiki/File:Hurricane_Evacuation_Route.jpg

Page 42:
Rappaport E. N. 1999, American Meteorology Society. 10-15 January 1999. 339-342.

The No-Nonsense Guide To Hurricane Safety

Other Books in the No-Nonsense Safety Guide Series

Published By Lulu Books & Beyond The Spectrum

The No-Nonsense Guide To Tornado Safety

• Paperback: 84 pages • Publisher: lulu.com (November 22, 2013) • Language: English • ISBN-10: 1304648648 • ISBN-13: 978-1304648648 • Product Dimensions: 9 x 6 x 0.2 inches • Shipping Weight: 6.4 ounce

The No-Nonsense Guide To Blizzard Safety

• Paperback: 54 pages • Publisher: lulu.com (December 21, 2013) • Language: English • ISBN-10: 9781304709394 • Product Dimensions: 9 x 6 x 0.2 inches • Shipping Weight: 0.28 pounds

The No-Nonsense Guide To Hurricane Safety

The No-Nonsense Guide To Flood Safety.

• Paperback: 60 pages • Publisher: lulu.com (November 22, 2013) • Language: English • ISBN-10: 1304648613 • Product Dimensions: 9 x 6 x 0.2 inches

The No-Nonsense Guide To Hurricane Safety.

• Paperback: 59 pages • Publisher: lulu.com (December 20, 2013) • Language: English • ISBN-10: 9781304733030 • Product Dimensions: 9 x 6 x 0.2 inches

Other upcoming books in the series include: "The No-Nonsense Guide to Fire Safety," The No-Nonsense Guide To Earthquake Safety," and "The No-Nonsense Guide To Automobile Safety."

The No-Nonsense Guide To Hurricane Safety

www.ingramcontent.com/pod-product-compliance
Lightning Source LLC
Chambersburg PA
CBHW020409290526
45785CB00005B/2477